"From monologues and elegies to first-person poetic prose pieces, José Angel Figueroa's *Heartbeats, Rhythms, And Fire* asks readers to question the origins of the self, the effects of intense hate, deeply-rooted love and the personas that come "before and beyond the chokehold of cries." Not only does Figueroa pull at the rhythms that vibrate from real people set as characters such as King Diamond and Almida, but he also relishes in the fight and fire created by activists such as Erica Garner and Oscar López Rivera. He pays homage to the agonizing genius and literary immortality of Julia de Burgos as only a founding member of the Nuyorican Poetry movement can. This collection of voices created by José Angel Figueroa is what remains when you "can't kill relentless faith born from the spirituals of stardust and many rivers."

—PEGGY ROBLES-ALVARADO,
Award-winning poet and editor of
Mujeres, The Magic, The Movement, and The Muse
and other collections

"José Angel time travels through poppy fields divined in the pauses between his shape shifting and spinning of *recuerdos*. He is a *piraguero* dousing the coldness of the world with the warmth of his empathic imagination."

—MAGDALENA GOMEZ,
Award-winning Poet, Playwright, Educator, and
Poet Laureate of Springfield, Massachusetts
(2019-2021)

"Poetry and Tales
Lead to a Sober Melody
Of Love and Life.
Words paint images of time
Gone and Coming.
They are Alive and Well.

José Angel Figueroa's
Craft and Style
Speaks sounds
Of Heat and Soul.

This poet knows
It is Where the moon
Goes when it is Blue.
GRAN!"

— AMINA BARAKA, Poet,
actress, author, community
organizer, singer, and dancer

"Master wordsmith José Angel Figueroa's new book, *Heartbeats, Rhythms, And Fire* makes us think beyond the words on the page. A poet who mysteriously connects words into dancing partners, expressing with grace, outrage, and affection, life's eternal emotions. His poetic songs are history telling, screaming with anger over human injustices. He teaches us to discover and listen to our own inner rhythms, and he does this while entertaining the heart and mind."

—GEORGE MALAVE,
Photographer and visual artist

"José Angel Figueroa's new poetry collection, *Heartbeats, Rhythms, And Fire* incorporates the voices of many oceans and crossroads. Here is poetry fully empowered by jazz-like rhythms that remind us of Coltrane in *A Love Supreme*. And it is LOVE, the thematic thrust that sparks the heartbeats of poetic fire in poems like, "Black Pearl," "Alma y Vida," "TRANSNIGHTIFICATION," "Poet Pedro Pietri, "The Immigrant's Tale," and "Oscar is Everywhere but Home," to name just a few. Each poem in the collection is a lesson of liberation that refuses to be subdued."

—PEDRO LÓPEZ ADORNO,
Poet, novelist, literary critic,
and anthologist

"*Heartbeats, Rhythms, And Fire* is a moving, reflective, evocative, and experiential collection of poems. José Angel Figueroa is a poet, uncompromising to truth, history, critical sanity, and way of life, humaneness, warmth and triumphant joy. This book is at the very heart of his life, soul, and vision. It's that inspiration and meaning that we all seek. For this visual artist, it's also that poetic voice of urgency, affirmation and meaning I seek in my own work. It's that Nuyorican Puerto Rican human spirit that insistently refuses to be colonized and dehumanized. Figueroa embraces all unheard brood in every dark corner of this God forsaken disconcerted world. Always filled with lucidity, love, refuge, respect, fulfillment and self-determination, Figueroa's poetry is his liberation... his rite of passage... the necessary revolution for us all."

—JUAN SÁNCHEZ,
Visual artist and Professor of Art, Hunter College
City University of New York

Other poetry works by José Angel Figueroa

The Invisibles (Coauthor George Malave)
Un Espejo En Mi Propio Bastidor
A Mirror In My Own Backstage
Hypocrisy Held Hostage
Noo Jork
East 110th Street
Unknown Poets from the Full-Time Jungle
Poets of Reason
Children's Language Sandwiches
As We Are
La Patria, The Homeland, Mi Tierra
Inner Self
The Visionary Poets
Dreams in a Famous Hotel
In Search of the Poet
Poetry: A Hunt for Imaginary Knowledge
Self-Xpression
Talking Pencils I and II
A Larger Reality in a Season of Truth
The Listener's Self I & II
White, Black & Brown Ice Cream Rhythms
YALA Journal I, II, III
(Young Adult Learning Academy)

HEARTBEATS, RHYTHMS, AND FIRE

HEARTBEATS, RHYTHMS, AND FIRE

José Angel Figueroa

Red Sugarcane Press, Inc.
New York, New York

Heartbeats, Rhythms, And Fire
Copyright © 2019 José Angel Figueroa

All rights reserved. No part of this publication may be reproduced, distributed or transmitted in any form or by any means, including photocopying, recording, or other electronic or mechanical methods, without the prior written permission of the publisher, except in the case of brief quotations embodied in critical reviews and other noncommercial uses permitted by copyright law. To request permission, write to publisher at:
info@RedSugarcanePress.com.

Publisher:
Red Sugarcane Press
534 West 112th Street #250404
New York, New York 10025
www.RedSugarcanePress.com

Editor & Book Layout: Iris Morales
https://irismoralesnyc.wordpress.com/

Cover and Interior Art: © Rudy Gutierrez
https://altpick.com/rudygutierrez

ISBN: 978-1-7340271-0-5 (Paperback)
ISBN: 978-1-7340271-1-2 (eBook)
Library of Congress Control Number: 2019914213

Printed in the United States of America
First Edition

Dedication

For Amiri Baraka (1934-2014)
The Last Poet Laureate of
New Ark, who was hip
to hypocrisy

And Walter Velez (1939–2018)
Art Illustrator & Graphic Designer

Contents

Foreword: Identities, Nations, and Literary Movements Dr. Melba Joyce Boyd	1
Reflections of a Scholar Dr. Alberto Martínez-Márquez	11

HEARTBEATS   17

Black Pearl	19
TRANSNIGHTIFICATION	21
Happy Face	23
Have Poet Will Travel	24
I N G E N U I T Y	25
O m i n o u s	27
Johnny Cool	28
The Child Who Took Time Apart	29
The Soul of Cyrano	36
Amorosa's Blues	39
The Gambling Philosopher	41
Mindless	43
Cross-Eyed Vagabond	45
An Enchanting Graveyard	46
Not All People Get Invited to Their Own Funeral	47
The Laughing Clock	48

RHYTHMS 51

Alma y Vida	53
King Diamond	56
Roseland Taxi Dancer	57
Don Juan de Lummox	60
Wind Dancer	61
Samba Pa' Mi	63
Poet Pedro Pietri	66
Prelude to An Exit	67
Sleeping With Guns	68
Devil's Orphan	69
Color Me Unique	70
Baby Grin	71
The Stand-By Effect	72
Enraged Rage	74
Love Insurance	76
Dark Hooded Phantom	77
"Love Always, Minnie"	79

AND FIRE 107

The Blood of the Poet	109
The Immigrant's Tale	114
The Undesirables & Unstoppable	115
Cool Chameleon	119
JULIA de JULIA	120
Aphrodite's Wisdom	123
Person #000	124
Mad Dog Blues	126
The Anonymous Thinker	128
Anatomy of Hatred	129
I am Erica Garner!	131

Oscar is Everywhere but Home	133
The Storm, the Hurricane and the Rebellion	136
La Tormenta, el Huracán y la Rebelión	142
Acknowledgements	149
About the Author	151
About the Artist	153
About the Editor	155
About Red Sugarcane Press	156

Foreword:
Identities, Nations, and Literary Movements

Heartbeats, Rhythms, And Fire is the latest of twenty-two books by José Angel Figueroa, an impressive bibliography for any writer but especially for one who writes in two languages for a range of communities and diverse audiences. In 1973, he published his first poetry book, *East 110th Street*, at Broadside Press. Since then, he has amassed a literary arsenal that has impacted and altered the limitations of the idea of American poetry as being Anglo and English.

"Heartbeats," "Rhythms," and "Fire" are also the thematic subtitles arranged with rich poems that contain American and European literary references and content, but José Angel encounters these realms with provocative counterpoints, reversals, and expansive meanings. At the same time, his unique style embraces contemporary issues with bravado and grace. José Angel's poetry engages the reader with wonder, insight, and surprise with a perspective that is grounded in the complex depths of an African/Taíno/Spanish heritage nurtured in the rich depths of barrios in Puerto Rico and New York, embellished by the challenges of life.

Historical Overview

When Dudley Randall established Broadside Press in 1965, it was the height of the Civil Rights Movement and the emergence of the Black Arts Movement, which inspired him to establish a poetry press to provide publishing opportunities for Black writers. In 1972, I joined the editorial staff; and, as the assistant editor, my duties included reviewing manuscripts and preparing galleys for the printer. A poetry manuscript by José Angel Figueroa, *East 110th Street*, stood out of hundreds that landed on my desk. I suggested to Randall, and he agreed, that we publish it. This decision coincided with another editorial decision by Jill Witherspoon Boyer to broaden the 1973 edition of *The Broadside Annual* by including Puerto Rican and Afro-Brazilian poets. Shortly thereafter, we agreed that the 1975 book, *Tengo*, poems by the Afro-Cuban poet Nicholas Guillen, translated into English by Richard Carr, should also be published, which further delineated that Broadside Press's literary mission needed to include Afro Latinx authors, who also faced discrimination in the mainstream publishing industry.

Through *East 110th Street*, Broadside Press intersected with the Nuyorican Poetry Movement and the cross-cultural connections between two movements occurring simultaneously, individually, and collectively. The convergence was a natural outgrowth of political circumstances in the United States and aesthetics that defied "art for art's sake." Reading José Angel's poetry, this cultural intersection is obvious. His political poetics and thematic perspectives give voice to his community in rhythms and imagery that resound and respond to sights and sounds from his points of origin and understanding. In tandem with José Angel's evolution as a poet within the context of what was happening in 1973 in Harlem, it is appropriate that this latest book is partially dedicated to

Amiri Baraka (1934-2014) who is regarded as a leader of the Black Arts Movement.

What was personally special about the publishing event of José Angel's first book was that I had the pleasure to meet and present *East 110th Street* to him in New York City. Randall thought it was a great idea for me to present José Angel's book in person. This trip also included attending a poetry concert in Central Park the next day featuring The Last Poets and meeting Nuyorican poet, Pedro Pietri.

Pietri appears in José Angel's latest book in a subtle and skillful tribute titled, "Poet Pedro Pietri." This poem simulates and encapsulates Pietri's style in language that Dudley Randall would identify as "sunken imagery," reflexive, deep-seated thought patterns that reverberate beneath, within, and between abstract phrases. José Angel describes the actions of his friend:

> He counts the number of
> dreams stray pigeons eat
> from insomniac travelers

The opening stanzas pose the poet in a seemingly tranquil image, but a single line disrupts this illusion with a warning:

> If you see Pedro sitting
> on any park bench
> watch out!

This element of disruption or the unexpected is likewise applicable to reading Pietri's poetry. In this poem, José Angel declares,

> Pedro rents coffins.
>
> Ask him, and he will tell you

> he just trains pigeons
> to bark at dogs.

Literary Consciousness

Heartbeats, Rhythms, And Fire opens with the poem "Black Pearl." The order and arrangement of the book are constructed to illustrate José Angel's literary consciousness, a complex ethnicity with Africa at the center and the beginning of his human identity:

> Heart-shaped Africa is the axis of
> My ancestral charcoal roots. I am
> A black pearl mixed with the dust
> Of a violet moon and brown
> Sugar babies baptized in fire.

José Angel poses the unspoken:

> Why does my
> Blackness still petrify you.
> Am I not the first daughter
> Of the night?

He talks back to power and conventions by offering alternative perspectives that challenge and deconstruct prevailing notions and values.

José Angel also interfaces mundane, everyday images with reversals that awaken perception. In "Mindless," he pronounces: "These are things you can't talk about in the office / Where the grumblers you work with / Hate their take-home pay / Cause it really doesn't / Take them home."

In other poems, José Angel's oeuvre contains classical allusions and subjects, but he reverses conventional perception of certain mythological characters, such as in "Don Juan de Lummox:

> Deep inside, Don
> Juan saw himself as a petrified half-wit,
> Who could not face the radiant princess
> Next door . . .

The poem peers into the insecurities that manifest in Don Juan's philandering:

> Dying for True Love,
> Minus the one
> Who got
> Away.

The poem's layout on the page leads to inevitability in meaning, creating a more rapid pace in the beginning that resolves into a slow stop. Likewise, "The Soul of Cyrano," as in Cyrano de Bergerac, considers another tragic character who "was exiled / To the moon when / Darkness came."

> This *ménage à trois* of love,
> blood and tears are the
> grandeur stages of poetry.

The poem "I am Erica Garner!" owns the power and the pain of "many lives / and a great-grand-daughter / of those conceived by rape." Written in the first person, "I," the poem traces the historical strength of Black women from cotton plantations through "the strong backbone / of Sojourner Truth and / wings of Harriet Tubman." This poem is the voice from "turbulent times" to the "chokehold crises of / Black Lives Matter." The shift from male to female voice is liberating on several levels, as it challenges the reader to embrace and to appreciate that the perspective of resistance and revolution are not primarily male actions but have also been a burden carried, birthed, and inspired by women.

A similar insight appears in a prose piece, "Love Always, Minnie," comprised of several short chapters, written in two voices, both in the first person. The poet speaks in the prelude about a forgotten occurrence and chance meeting with a friend's sister. A photograph provides the evidence, but what is moving about the piece is that José Angel writes in the voice of a young woman diagnosed with cancer; and, by assuming this perspective, he expresses sensitivity that is nuanced and takes the audience into a female space. This gender shift provides a thematic narrative that also requires the reader to assume another point of view and possibly consciousness.

José Angel's sense of brotherhood is reflected in "Samba Pa' Mi," and the disturbing imagery lingers long after the reading ends. The internal musings of the poet:

> I've known grief and sorrow
> with the chords of anger
> and tortuous seasons
> of blind complicity.

The poem is a poignant retelling of an encounter with a junkie, dying in an alley, "Stealing himself from me." "Looking at his head / Nodding like Coltrane / Rhythms." The thoughts of futility drive the poem and the poet's grief.

> I never got home that night
> cause my Brother left me
> to walk alone while he was
> stolen from the world.

"The Storm, the Hurricane And the Rebellion" is appropriately the last poem in the book, included in both English and Spanish. It revisits the natural disaster, "Maria," that devastated the landscape and the people of Puerto Rico. The epigram is a quote from Zora Neale

Hurston's *Their Eyes Were Watching God.* "Don't you realize that the sea is the home of water," which is a reminder about the natural essence and dominant element of our planet. José Angel contrasts the apolitical power of nature with the vicious responses of the island's governor and the president of the United States:

> A natural disaster wouldn't know
> if the tears of the skies could be
> wiped by flying paper towels.
>
> María had no idea the global power
> elite built wars in your backyard
> or that the Jones Act made Puerto Rico
> an American cash cow.
>
> What POTUS called a great rescue
> mission, we call a flea market of
> bonds reduced to junk status
> for U.S. millionaires licensed
> to kill the poor.

The spirit of this poem reiterates José Angel's commitment to truth and praises the people for taking action and rebuking racist and classist politicians. Poetry may have many purposes, but the one that aspires to open the eyes and minds of the public is courageous, and it is the voice that has frightened the powers-that-be since Plato's Republic. The final stanzas proclaim:

> People united in a revolutionary
> awakening so that our voices
> would no longer be silenced
> or pushed into exile.
>
> La Patria rose and it refused
> to be Puertoricanless!

"Somos más y no tenemos miedo."

¡Que viva Puerto Rico libre!

Afterword

José Angel's poetry moves in and out of worlds, from neighborhoods into professional settings. His poems tell stories, recount histories, exclaim, and expose political outrage.

The recognition of the African Diaspora in the Caribbean and South America as a multi-racial, complex ethnicity is an aesthetic aspect that emerged in the United States during the Harlem Renaissance in the creative expressions of Langston Hughes, Jean Toomer, Claude McKay, and Zora Neale Hurston, among others. Their global consciousness spoke to the challenge that W. E. B. DuBois predicted in *The Souls of Black Folk*:

> The problem of the twentieth century is the problem of the color line—the relation of the darker to the lighter races of men in Asia and Africa, in America and the islands of the sea.

The colonization of Puerto Rico by Spain brought enslaved Africans and indigenous Caribbean people into another historical intersection, producing a new world cultural evolution. The subsequent possession of the island by the United States resulted in Puerto Ricans migrating particularly to New York's Harlem. Their racialized circumstances entered another configuration of oppression, and their poets conjured a new American literature in the cadence of Spanish blended into English through the lens of an African/Taíno/Spanish culture that generated amazing voices that have rendered dynamic poetics, reverberating above and beyond geopolitical color lines.

José Angel Figueroa is a stellar voice in a constellation of poets who defy and redefine the color line by reassigning meaning to imagery and complicating sounds that refuse to be muffled, ignored or silenced by English or stifled by Castilian Spanish. As José Angel illustrates and reiterates throughout his poetry, "the border crossed over me." This poet gives the world an expansive range of themes that sometimes exposes the language and cultural practices of hypocrisy, and, in other instances, juxtaposes tragedy with tenderness, or strength and resilience, resisting tyranny and ignorance.

In every instance, José Angel's poetry is nuanced, dynamic, and brilliant.

DR. MELBA JOYCE BOYD

Dr. Boyd is a Distinguished Professor in the Department of African American Studies at Wayne University in Detroit and an Adjunct Professor in Afroamerican and African Studies at the University of Michigan, Ann Arbor. An award-winning author of thirteen books and more than 100 essays, she is also a documentary filmmaker. Her poetry, essays, and creative nonfiction have appeared in anthologies and other publications in the United States and Europe, and her work has been recognized with numerous awards. Her latest poetry collection, *Death Dance of a Butterfly* received the 2013 Library of Congress Notable Books Award for Poetry.

Boyd is the author of "This Museum Was Once a Dream," the official poem engraved on the wall of the Wright Museum of African American History. Her critically acclaimed and widely reviewed *Discarded Legacy: Politics and Poetics in the Life of Frances*

E.W. Harper, 1825-1911 (1994) was the first comprehensive study of Harper. Boyd was a Fulbright Scholar at the University of Bremen and has a Doctor of Arts in English from the University of Michigan, and M.A. and B.A. degrees in English from Western Michigan University.

Reflections of a Scholar

The literary career of José Angel Figueroa has been intrinsically linked to the neo-Rican and nuyorican movement, an intellectual, literary, and cultural movement emerging in New York City in the 1960s. Puerto Rican artists, poets, playwrights, and writers who were born or raised in the United States created a powerful literary movement and tradition that defied and challenged the institutional invisibility and oppression of the Puerto Rican people. Navigating two cultures and two languages, their works described experiences with migration, racism, and poverty, and gave voice to struggles for social justice and equality. This literary movement birthed a new cultural identity and language of resistance for Puerto Ricans who came of age in New York and still remained connected to a colonized island.

José Angel Figueroa's poetry originates from this tradition. His poetics linked to the performativity of the word that seeks to transcend circumstances and transform into an emancipatory force. A key characteristic of his poetry is its conversational tone through which he creates a regenerating dialogue with history, culture, and the poetry itself.

José Angel's *Heartbeats, Rhythms, And Fire* is an innovative departure in the work of this exceptional poet. This new collection is divided into three parts referenced by the title itself. "Heartbeats" represents the dynamic spirit or vital impulse constant in the human experience, extending beyond the physical environment to include emotions. "Rhythms" embodies the variability of life's experiences, and their unique and random character. The last section, "And Fire," encompasses the principle of energy moving toward individual or societal transformation that is authentic and responsible.

Heartbeats, Rhythms, And Fire is distinguished from José Angel's previous works in which the specific experience of the Puerto Rican Diaspora is more prevalent. This does not mean that it is abandoned—rather this collection presents a range of themes and styles. His poetry is imbued with a cadence and tempo that emulate jazzy compositions without giving up his social commitments. The jazz motif sets the cadencious structure of the poetry inscribed as a tuning fork from which a revealing and redemptive word is transmitted as can be seen in "TRANSNIGHTIFICATION:"

> But when cool jazz
> bathed her thighs
> in prophecy
>
> She married nature
> & met her mind
> With the allure of
>
> Truth & beauty from
> The wisdom of
> Deep-rooted trees

On the other hand, the poet serves as an intermediary between the world of experience (*lebenswelt*) and the creative act (*dichtung*). The poet emerges as a spokesperson for humanity that lives in the vortex of this "theater of situations." Therefore, the poetry is born from the social context itself—that is where the word derives its essential vitality while still being supported by lyrical impulse.

In the opening poem titled, "Black Pearl," the implicit poet or poetic voice expresses, not without a hint of nostalgia, the following:

> My voice is the bitter cry of many
> Oceans and crossroads. My tears
> Are uprooted trees longing to
> Return to sacred firewater.

Later in the poem, the implicit poet manifests as a transformative agent. Precisely, the use of calamity accentuates the idea of change and mutability, as can be read below:

> I have torn down that massive
> Veil which made me feel my
> Existence was once a problem.
>
> I will not bend. Be harnessed.
> Kept silent. Be forbidden to
> Bear my own fruits or dance
> With the constellations.

There is a *Heideggerian* echo in it that reminds us of the idea of concealment through which the true being is accessed.

To conclude, the intertextual record of *Heartbeats, Rhythms, And Fire* is not limited to music and jazz as in the poems, "The Blood of the Poet," "Samba Pa' Mi," and "Mad Dog Blues." The collection is a comprehensive poetic record consisting of a broad mix of classical and modern literary references, such as Cyrano de Bergerac, Venus, Athena, Prometheus, and Don Juan. There are also portrayals and allusions to real persons, such as Julia de Burgos, Pedro Pietri, Oscar López Rivera, Erica Garner, Sojourner Truth and Harriet Tubman who have earned a place in history, as well as descriptions of anonymous personalities and fictitious characters who we encounter throughout our lives. The poem, "Oscar is Everywhere but Home," dedicated to the former Puerto Rican political prisoner López Rivera, stands out. A section of the poem follows:

> Why was this "Mandela of the
> Americas" so dangerous to
> The U.S. penal wastelands
> And its toxic existence?
>
> Because Oscar refused
> to be on his knees
> *¡Cuando los cogió*
> *con la mano en la masa!*
>
> Gringolandia was caught
> Red-handed in the act
> Of colonial oppression!
>
> A bona fide revolutionary
> Can't be neutralized or
> Rehabilitated, America!

Heartbeats, Rhythms, And Fire by José Angel Figueroa boldly weaves a lyrical universe that gives us rhythms and cadences, an "emotional passport" to new directions, far from the spiritual genocide and tyranny of humanity, to an understanding where we continue being "a labor of love / In progress."

DR. ALBERTO MARTÍNEZ-MÁRQUEZ

Dr. Martínez-Márquez is the Chair of the Department of Humanities at the University of Puerto Rico in Aguadilla and a visiting professor at la Universidad del Sagrado Corazón in Santurce. Martínez Márquez is a poet, narrator, playwright, essayist, amateur photographer, artisan, and performer. He has published approximately twenty poetry books and is a 1987 recipient of the prestigious Francisco Matos Paoli Poetry Medal. His work has appeared in national and international magazines, journals, and anthologies.

Martínez-Márquez belongs to the renowned generation of writers of the 1980s in Puerto Rico characterized by social and literary projects, and counter discourse against powerful elites. He coauthored with Mario R. Cancel an anthology of poets from this period called "El límite volcado" (2000), which received a PEN award in Puerto Rico. Since 2003, he has directed "Letras Salvajes / Wild Letters," an online cultural magazine that serves as a link among Latinx voices.

HEARTBEATS

Black Pearl

Heart-shaped Africa is the axis of
My ancestral charcoal roots. I am
A black pearl mixed with the dust
Of a violet moon and brown
Sugar babies baptized in fire.

My rose-purple lips praise
The faith of my grandmothers
Whose sweet, salty and pungent
Heartstrings never cracked when
Singing the Black Folks' blues.

My voice is the bitter cry of many
Oceans and crossroads. My tears
Are uprooted trees longing to
Return to sacred firewater.

My soul is entombed with the
Allure of lavender pouring
From the gifts of dawn.

I have torn down that massive
Veil which made me feel my
Existence was once a problem.

I will not bend. Be harnessed.
Kept silent. Be forbidden to
Bear my own fruits or dance
With the constellations.

My thunderous heart will turn
White sparks into a hot glare.
My story will be told without
The putrid disgust of hatred.

Africa did not make an
Outcast out of me.

Why does my Blackness
Still petrify you.
Am I not the first daughter
Of the night?

TRANSNIGHTIFICATION

When she saw herself
in the mirror the
wallflower wearing

Folksy white with
grass growing wild
between her toes

Made an appearance

But when cool jazz
bathed her thighs
in prophecy

She married nature
& met her mind
with the allure of

Truth & beauty from
the wisdom of
deep-rooted trees

She hummed those
crevices, swirled her
bones & swam in fire

She danced before the
onset of darkness
at the end of day

& gave birth to an
afterglow of history
when she found Earth

Just a moment ago

Happy Face

Happy's peace of mind and
Lighted-hearted smile swam
In sync with the solace and
Eyes of a special child

Enjoying a gust of wind in
The sounds of nature and
Blessings of remembrance
With unbridled freedom

When Happy gazed into the
Abyss it did not make him
Unwise when he failed to see
Strangers act like rubber
Souls with heartburn

His imagination was magical -
Living, laughing, loving
That moment you befriend
The spirit of humanity as
The season of a lifetime

And make the world
Your goodwill neighbor
With a gracious hello

Have Poet Will Travel

I am not responsible where
    my thoughts go when I'm
feeling like cool mint and a
    midnight blues eclipsed in
a thunderous silence.

    I am dangerously in love
       with every possibility
    and its creation to probe
    if we are all born of
amorous times or fear.

    I refuse to jam with boring
       nightwalkers whose
    nomadic rhythms spiral
       like splintered clouds.

    Every night has its own
       morning glory with its
    lush rhapsody waiting
       for the next dance
to taste heaven.

    I no longer wander in the
       shades and grasp of
my earthly sorrows.

    Perhaps I'm an orphan
    of the universe —
primitive and soulful

       —Just like you.

INGENUITY

I was born an oddity and
am proud of my inner gifts,
always taking it one step
further and beyond.

The most beautiful tormentors
once confessed my outlook
drove them frenzied. But I
knew they died of envy.

I am the counterpart of an
elastic mind freelancing with
kaleidoscopic reality. I can get
to the moon by sleepwalking.
I can listen to a grain of sand
from a desert of loneliness
and write cosmic prayers
to befriend my soul.

My thinking may be unusual
but I am not a numskull who
uses his luminous smile as a
mirror to ignite my own light.

I have a penchant to dance
with the constellations of
chaos, love and purpose to
resolve the mystery of why
human nature is colorful.

Observe. Seek knowledge.
Question the ultimate truth.
Listen with acuity. Absorb.

Connect to art and swim
in the aesthetic dreams
of the imagination.

You must risk madness
to reach the seashores
of ingenuity.

Ominous

I was once a crestfallen
star who was exiled to
Earth by the Winged
Messenger of Mercury

I was a cantankerous spirit
Who hated Nature when it
Whispered its secrets to
The solace of the winds

Eons later my alien rump
was unearthed by a blind
old sage from a forest
long frozen in oblivion

She read my rogue silence
like a talking mirror
and called me Ominous

This oracle lived in harmony
with fire loving the simplest
things most misguided fools
mourned or craved for

I was plunged into nightfall
and arose from darkness
when she had healed
my apocalyptic ways

With the mystical libido
of the moon while I
discovered the poetic
labyrinth of the soul

Johnny Cool

My face was inspired by true events.

I walk among the anonymous
As a sublime remembrance
From some yesterday.

Let's not pretend
You don't see me.

I was once all of you always
Playing the opposite so that
No one could ever see what
Emotions looked like when

You decorated your face
With a blank stare.

You aged me with doubts
When it was raining envy
Inside you and I unmasked

My face to return home
To my own skin.

I'm no longer that roadside
Lover who ponders the
Loneliness of his soul.

The Child Who Took Time Apart

*"Time is the parental element of our beginning;
it is the blue algae of dreaming."*
— Claudia Hammond, Time Warped

Venus brought Adam peace and tranquility
As his moonflower and love goddess until
A heartbreak of silent grief ate him
When Venus died the moment
Their daughter Athena was born.

Death claimed Venus' life to remind
The living that not everything truly
Happens at once and lasts forever.

Yet to depart is the doorway
To another journey where
Nothing is uncertain.

Adam drifted in nirvana blues
When living seemed like a
Prolonged curse as the days grew
Bitter clouds and sorrow.

For Athena's sake, Papa asked
Grandpa Essen to move in while
He struggled to let go of Venus'
Aroma and make fresh plans
For this big-eyed child who
Danced with her hands.

Grandpa and Papa came from
The same blood but lived in
Different planets. One was a
Jaded scientist and the other,
A grief-stricken zombie.

Grandpa and Athena were inseparable.

He painted her ceiling and walls in
A mist of sky-blue glimmering with
Twilight stars and the Milky Way.

Athena loved his wild tales of
The fabric of a cosmic orchestra
Where timekeepers from ancient
Worlds kept the secrets of the dead.

Grandpa worshiped her whirlwind
Imagination as if she lived in
A realm outside of time itself.

He reminisced when Athena created
A childhood sandcastle and invited
Majestic butterflies, leaping frogs,
Baby turtles and acrobatic hamsters
Who ran in circles to celebrate her
12th birthday at exactly 12 noon.

Papa warned quixotic Grandpa not
To give Athena unicorns, dragons,
Sea horses or lazy-bone dinosaurs.

Instead, he gave her a vintage clock
The size of a silver dollar that was
As unique and spellbinding as she.

Athena held the delicate timepiece
And felt its gold-tinged circumference,
Put it close to her ears and heard
Its heart beat as if it were human.

From this very moment, this
Big-eyed child wanted to know
If time was a prisoner in a
Prism of memories as elusive
As the spoken winds.

"I created this cesium clock, "declared
Grandpa. "It's so precise that in
The next sixty million years,
It will never gain or lose a second."

Enchanted, Athena asked,
"How long is a second, Grandpa?"

"This replica beats 9 billion, 192 million,
631 thousand, 770 oscillations that is
The precise length of a second, my child."

"You're so full of fishtails and
Spinning windmills, Grandpa!"

Laughing, he replied, "Place it gently
Under your SpongeBob SquarePants pillow
And many stories will swim in your dreams."

"Will I remember them?" asked Athena.

"Only those memories worth keeping,
My child. A day is not exactly
Twenty-four hours when Earth's
Rotation slows down over time."

"Then how long is today?" she inquired.

"It depends on faith, love, and hope,
My dear. These are the rhythms of
Our consciousness," he sighed.

"Why, Grandpa? Tell me more!"

Smiling and in awe, Grandpa replied,
"These emotions are the winged
Songs of earthly prayers."

"What if you're a poor optimist, Grandpa?"

"Daring to wonder," he replied, "is not
A hopeless dream. Nor is science
Always the best answer."

"Why, Grandpa?" Athena pondered.

"Because the future does not wear
Old shoes. Time clicks its heels in
Divine meditation and immortal
Inspiration," he prophesized.

"Like dreams drifting on water, Grandpa."

"Exactly, my little genius! I must go now."

Grandpa grew tired and began
To exit before it struck midnight
When the hands of time flew
Between Nature's beauty
And its unforgiving terror.

"Where are you going, Grandpa?"

"A poem is creeping up behind me,"
He winked, "and if I don't write it,
My mind becomes a blank page."

Grandpa reminded Athena when he
Doesn't write, his fierce battle with
Insomnia becomes a mousetrap.

"Will you return to see me, Grandpa?"

"Of course, my treasure. You're
The reason why I've ceased
To be chained to guilt and
Pathos, like Prometheus."

"Like Papa?" she inquired.

"Papa may be in a deep hole now,"
He replied. "But his dim spark
Will come to us as a new flame."

With those last words, Grandpa
Made himself invisible.

Come 12 midnight, Athena
Dismantled Grandpa's precious
Gift and set time free from its
Gilded cage. It was no longer
Trapped in our hands.

This pendulum of pins, nuts, bolts,
Arrow hands and a dial was gutted and
Stood naked with no more seconds
Waiting for a minute to be the
Breaking news story of the hour.

Grandpa Essen was not horrified
Or panicked if time was unreal,
Now that Athena took it apart.

Here today, gone tomorrow,
He thought.

Athena was the daughter of Venus:
The goddess in every woman who saw
Time as a flame-keeper to enlighten
old knowledge and make
That promise of loving a sacred
Blessing out of nowhere.

Knowing time could rest in peace
Behind an Unknown Epitaph
Written in glorious tears:

Where the sun and the moon
And its siblings the stars
Once met and gave the
Universe its first
Taste of water.

The Soul of Cyrano

"How Fate loves a jest!"
-Cyrano de Bergerac,
   By Edmond Rostand

The cavalier poet and master
swordsman fought a hundred
duels to defend his panache
and the beauty of the soul.

But it was an old nemesis
— Vanity — that had the last
laugh when death gave
Cyrano a crowning hour

To see his beloved Roxanne.

Despite Cyrano's grotesque
proboscis, his swordplay
struck awe and terror in
the face of the elite while

The poet charmed himself.

His triumph was in putting
enchanting words in the
trembling lips of his rival:
a tongue-tied heartthrob

Whose soul was written
in his perfumed eyes.

Roxanne's frivolous beauty
was of a harlequin who
played to the illusions of
heartstrings and regrets.

Each was a *nom de plume*
of forlorn comic tragedy
and masterful understudy
in their own backstage.

This virtuous farce began when
these star-crossed romantics
were absorbed by unrequited
love hidden in falsehood.

What appeared to be was
the mask of ambiguity
to camouflage the liaison.

Only Christian was true to
his swashbuckling desires
while Cyrano and Lady
Love played flawlessly

The art of beguiling fools.

This handsome devil was
used as a cosmetic pawn in
a pompous cock game of
beau geste and deception.

Cyrano fed the peacock
moonlighting wit to charm
Roxanne's soul and swoon
like a spoiled sparrow.

Not all lies are ugly
or brute failures.

No wonder she loved
only one man and
lost him twice.

Poor Cyrano was
exiled to the moon
when darkness came.

This *ménage à trois* of love,
blood and tears are the
grandeur stages of poetry.

Amorosa's Blues

Please don't be a bitter
sweet lemon tonight

I'm feeling nice and
mellow sinking my
mind out of time and
deep into this pillow

Don't put your silk-
spoken appetite on me
like some aqua marine

Peddling the moon at
a moment's notice so
I could loan you the sea

To live on when yearning
to see your face buried
in my sacred yoni

When you're listening
to the tapping of mice
dancing to dusty dead

Songs and the last
drops of an empty
bottle of wine

Please be kind and
don't bite and taste like
a bitter lemon, tonight

My Love Rose:
I am immune
to your diet

The Gambling Philosopher

Spoiler Alert: falling in love
    is an oxymoron!

I am a gambling philosopher
    with a poetic theory known
to write little masterpieces
    in midair. Warning: If you
are the amorphous type

Who looks for love in the
    supermarket and selects
a significant other like
    squeezing fresh fruits
or organic vegetables

This poem is not for you.

If you're not happy with
    what you have, you may
have lost it way before
    it was gone if you treat
love like a used car.

Fall for an alluring mixed nut
    who hunts for blank verse
like a flytrap and you grow
    old much too young with
popcorn stuck in your teeth.

Safer to fly-in-love beyond
    these accolades of deceit
sans the erotic erudition
    flapping on your feet.

It demands listening to the
    rhythms of a dancing guitar
with an emotional passport

To a blessed miracle without
    a parachute in your pocket.

Mindless

you know you are on edge
but don't want to think
when it's one of those days
you're losing a lot of things

and instead withdraw by
doing little nothings to
walk in timeless waters

while my inamorata who
is close yet so far gently
reminds me I still don't
know what love is

some people are in your
life forever while others
have an expiration date

it was simpler when a fly
on the wall could bug you
like an irritating lover

now you must beware
of wilted souls whose
desires break bones

and of humans who
speak to machines as
if they were pets

these are things you can't
talk about in the office
where the grumblers

you work with hate
their take-home pay
cause it really doesn't
take them home

so, the less you complain
the younger you remain

I just need my body to
catch up with my mind
so that I can think
out-of-the-box and sleep
with the sky!

Cross-Eyed Vagabond

ever had one of those days
when you don't know
where you are and see
weird things happening

in the middle of a herd of
tourists and you're so
lost you can't find

the rest of your body?

An Enchanting Graveyard

When I'm under fickle clouds that
Can't decide to cry or scream
Over the whims of gravity
To restore my faith and
Perhaps feel younger.

I drift across an enchanting
Graveyard where the departed
Rest among the solemn and
Fade like a mellow whisper
Wearing the nightfall.

I came to pay my respects
But they — the Quietus — were
Starving for my imagination
And said: Earthly dreams are

The artist's secret lover when
Passions were raindrops of fresh
Joy and grandiose lamentations
Served fearlessly with a crisp
Palate of insatiable desires.

As I exited this journey from
The uncertain I came upon
An epitaph that read:

Though My Thoughts Drift
My Ashes Lay Where
Love Is Pure Insomnia

Not All People Get Invited to Their Own Funeral

I smile because not all people get
    Invited to their own funeral

Most get the news before they knew
    Their time was uprooted when
Civic strangers dressed in scrub
    Injected chemicals in their brain

And spoke with the dead to describe
    That empty space when a loved
One enters our life to transform the
    Winds of self in others before
Passing onwards in our deepest
    Memories of promised vows
And fate mixed with expectations

As if life was some lazy afternoon
    Of nostalgic yesterday when
Universal kisses were heaven and
    You ordered breakfast in bed
And a mortician showed up instead!

Who am I? I am that sole witness to
    This crumbling – the dark truth
Of a two-faced shadow of light

When you woke up feeling quite odd
    All day and whispered – *Oh, Shit!*

The key to knowing is opening
    Your eyes!

The Laughing Clock
for Safijah

Time is a blessing

When not wasted like
Water pouring from
An open faucet

If you have forgotten
The rhythms of the
World you live in

All else is a wasteland
Ancient mountains of
Icebergs-in-motion for
Climate-change skeptics

If you can't you won't
And the failure to try
Is the worst defeat

Those who undermine
Organic beauty will
Turn envy into disbelief

Slay the naysayers who
Shake your hand and
Stab you with the other

Ambiguity is
Relentless retreat

Listen to the heartbeat of
The stars be unfulfilled
Desire and aim higher

Slay the naysayers with
Will power and laugh as
If time is blazing with

Revolution on
Your birthday!

RHYTHMS

RHYTHMS

Alma y Vida

for Doña Almida

When you blend *Alma y Vida*, you
beget *Almida:* The resolute soul of
a mother's tale of sacrifice, love
and struggle from the moment
she was born to the cradle in end
of life care. Though home spun

Almida lost her parents at an early
age and was forced to abandon
the fantasy of grammar before
she could unlock the secrets of
the universe and gazed at the
moon of forbidden desires to
whisper the tender things in
the tribulations of first love.

She possessed the indigenous
foresight in the school of life
and rose to a matting chorus of
coquis, coffee beans and maví.

She crocheted and cooked
yucca, calabaza and yams
before the roosters sang
to worship the sunrise.

*Almida fue una atrevida neo-
críolla de corazón Boricua
que tenía la sabiduría de la
cepa pura de nuestra patria.*

*Y para mí – Una maestra de
gran bendición sagrada!*

She was a daughter of the winds
who flew with shrewd wings
from this Enchanted Isle in a
gilded era of romantic boleros,
sweet mangoes, avocado trees
and the flamboyán rhythms of
Caribbean sugarcane dreams.

Almida came to the Big Apple
where this siren worked as
a seamstress and dared to
refine the brute coldness of
English with a spoonful
of amazing grace.

She could take the worst of
back-breaking nights that
rarely sang songs of respite
in her name or collected in
nostalgic family albums of
shared precious moments
embellished with humor
and blessings of gratitude.

Alma y Vida could hide the
tears that refused to die
in homemade sorrow to
protect you from the rain of
nagging doubt and snow
of remorse and pain.

Almida's triumphant spirit
came in the glory of faith, the
passion of stubborn persistence
and the fragrance of lilacs and
quiet wisdom she brought into
the heart of the living room.

To instill in her trailblazing
daughters and cyberspace
offspring the gifts of self-
reliance, humility, and free-
thinking Caribbean dreams.

King Diamond

King Diamond told me he
was a Jamaican stowaway
who came to Spanish Harlem
to get a Puerto Rican suntan.

He was this pit-bull dandy who
walked about with fire-engine
red threads like he owned the
rhythms of street traffic

And dared you not to laugh
at his wild stories.

King had very few things to
beam about after his parents
left him laying bare on the cold-
blooded steps of a police station.

"I was born a rough diamond
during an earthquake," he said.
"When two remorseful souls who
cursed the Lord for not baking
their own, had adopted me."

They took him home like some
leftover sandwich but made him
feel like a king before seeking
his rose in Spanish Harlem.

Roseland Taxi Dancer

I am unknown in a madcap
Crowd in Roseland where
Loneliness is the most
Popular stranger wearing

The true face of a lie

Playing taxi dancer
For the blues

I dance with you when
No one can get in your
Head once you are

Out of reach
Out of town
Out of sight
Out of mind

I have embraced those
Whose quest for perfection
Got lost in the city lights
Of a snowstorm before
The blink of an eye

I listen to the woes of those
Who squandered cherished
Kisses with ingratiated
Flattery and hype

You can't get everything
By giving nothing but
I will love you only
When we dance

Be it swing or bolero
A fearless waltz or
A seductive tango

Your mood swings
Are my songs

The musicians were tripping
In their own groove and
Went deep where jazz is
The epiphany of poetry

I snapped out of this
Razzmatazz when my
Lover beckoned and I
Was no longer at war

With myself

How profound to be without
Sound when someone with
Wit knows your worth

Was it that fire when
She blessed me with
Her burning desires

Whispering, "Return
Home, where your
Sea legs belong."

And I, a seagull, old as
Stale bread, smiled
Like a lovable pirate.

Don Juan de Lummox

A handsome rogue to some, a thief of hearts to so many others, a scoundrel to most, Don Juan grew up on sword and sandal flicks. He played the irrepressible charmer with aplomb by mastering the art of seducing the world's treasures. Deep inside, Don Juan saw himself as a petrified half-wit who could not face the radiant princess next door. A stutterer in his teens who wore second-hand clothes while cruising the Arabian nights with champagne dreams on a cabin's boy wages, Don Juan discovered a magical mirror. He put on a lavish fedora, shed the appearance of the jester and wrote sweet, resourceful words for the exotic splendor of dying for True Love, minus the one who got away.

Wind Dancer

Watching her move
Made my eyes flirt
With her rhythms

While my mind
Parachuted over
Her climate

Sinking her head
Deep in the pillow
She glanced at
My hungry mind

Kissing her moist
Lips, plucking them,
Nibbling as groans
Ripped open the
Spitfire of night

As she glided back
Pushing my mid-
Finger against her
Trembling, loving
Lower lip

My tongue was filled
With her aroma while
She was erupting in
Earthly splendor, silk
And blessed silence

"¡*Coño, Mami,* you're
A wind dancer!"

And her smile touched
Me *Goodnight* while
Hoping for a rerun

Samba Pa' Mi

After a spin of a cocktail head
dancing in midair I fade into
the mysteries of the night as
my soul is drifting home.

I was mellow yet forlorn
observing how the unseen
riding the subterranean
blues struggle to belong.

I've known grief and sorrow
with the chords of anger
and tortuous seasons
of blind complicity.

I was desperate to fly above
these unforgiving winds
and escape the politics
of bad memories.

My mother's stories of
living a fulfilling life
taught me to survive
the cynic's poison.

I learned if the world was
not waiting for you then
what is your purpose?
On my way home I heard
a cry from a shadow
where lack of faith was
a shattered mirror.

It came from a dark alley
stained with urine and
I saw this Youngblood
stealing himself from me.

Afraid, snap-back, staring
through the blackness in a
fetus position and hunger
that clamped his rib cage.

His eyes long dead before
his youth dried up against
the thick air, he sneaked
snail-like toward me.

Saying *nada,* he turned
his back and with hands
roped around his face,
crawled deep into night.

"*¡Diablo! Diablo! Diablo!*"
he screamed and with
fear stuck to my throat
I blurred, "Take it light."

He slammed his raging
fist on the brick wall,
knucklebones bleeding
trying to bite his veins.

"Help me! Help me!"
my Brother cried and I
feeling sick and empty
walk like a cat at prey

Looking at his head nodding
like Coltrane rhythms
trying to touch the ground.

His negro hair sweated like
grass in winter and skull
crashed like a hammer
knocking a nail in midair.

My armpits rained cause
I didn't know how to
hold death in my arms
wishing I was that alley

To comprehend the brutal
darkness he was in before
he waved his hands and
pushed me into silence.

I never got home that night
cause my Brother left me
to walk alone while he was
stolen from the world.

Poet Pedro Pietri

If you see Pedro sitting
        on any park bench
          watch out!

He counts the number of
        dreams stray pigeons eat
        from insomniac travelers
      passing by with lost weekends
        buried in torn pockets.

The poet sits there in black
funeral clothes and a Spanish
shopping bag full of anti-HIV
condoms and cosmic poems
singing doo wop during

The echoes of undertakers
        chewing gum over reality.

Pedro rents coffins.

Ask him, and he will tell you
        he just trains pigeons
          to bark at dogs.

Prelude to An Exit

When Mama knew her time
Was coming to a drip
She made this suggestion:

Why not simply throw
My cadaver in the ocean
And let the sharks enjoy
The rhythms of my bones.

She was always beyond
Her time until tomorrow
Could not wait for her.

I would read her poetry
With salty tears and shared
Colorful Caribbean folktales
Of how children learned to
Outwit the devil with charm
Without losing their faith
In human nature until she
Smiled and craved for dawn
To close her eyes.

All I want, she whispered, is
For you to outlive my nostalgia
And visit my grave with
A poem newly born.

Sleeping With Guns

"Bud" wasn't that high school prince
Who drove cheerleaders crazy
He stood out but was ignored

Unless you saw him nowhere
Fishing for random thoughts
And off the beaten track

He was an obnoxious clown
From the Bible Belt of bitter
Prayers and a six-pack where

Freethinking was a felony

"Bud" was a proud college dropout
Who graduated with honors
In chronic procrastination.

He left his childhood in the
Cornfields of wasted dreams
Where life is redemption

As long as you love
Sleeping with guns

Devil's Orphan

It was obvious he was offbeat
in outlook with the face
of an owl and sloping beak
matching prickly horns.

To stare at him and freeze
in quiet despair one may
pray his slanted eyes were
not the kiss of death.

The holy nuns who knew demons
loved dysfunctional souls
from sin city could only dare
to get stoned with him
and beg for forgiveness.

The puffed-up elitists and
hedonists craved to take him
to their mansions and play
kinky sex games to kill
the deluxe boredom.

The homeless saw him as
a vagabond saint drifting
like a mist of comic relief
and silly deathbed regrets.

The misogynist would hook
him up with his crazy sister
and make them a twosome.

Color Me Unique

Living in a world among
the vogue is akin to residing in
an avant-garde penthouse asylum
with sleepwalkers recovering from
a stubborn prom date with death.

I am unique. No, not a misfit
for the uncouth who prefer
I play some prissy ballerina
to reduce their emotional
constipation while they
wear Wall Street pajamas.

I am not afraid to conquer
behemoths with ugly toes
resembling small brains
in corporate boardrooms

Branding me:
Promiscuous Diva.

Baby Grin

My parents waited years before
I could smile. Everyone screamed
like wounded prisoners of war.
Mom never came out of the
kitchen. Pop froze in silence.

They were so old in their
ways they could bore
my pet turtle to death.

My childhood was a cactus plant
in the family album. I was forced
to glow with deep joy as if
a dashing prince kissed me.

I preferred goofy boys who spoke
with a secret smile and said less
in the face of anger. My baby
grin vanished their anxieties.

The first boy I kissed felt like
squirrels were eating my brain.

I am weird and beautiful,
always uplifting people who
feel like human coat hangers.

I may not look like
a sunflower but I am
truly a fascinating sunset.

The Stand-By Effect

For Kitty Genovese: 1935 -1964.[1]

Walking, running or even limping
you see too many heads isolated
from their shoulders, moving
through urban decay under

Blank dreams into retired days
and nervous breakdowns

People branching off from them-
selves further and furthermore
and it happens e-v-e-r-y day

A young woman, this time gets stalked,
raped and killed and a-g-a-i-n the
BREAKING NEWS, the shock and
invalid standby glances crashing
on cracked pavements

Mouths open! Eyes get pregnant
and everyone is the father, the
mother and that ill-fated child

---

1. Kitty Genovese, 28 years old, was brutally murdered and raped by a psychopath on March 13, 1964. Neighbors who heard her cries or saw the attack did nothing to help her. Abraham Michael Rosenthal details the account in *Thirty-Eight Witnesses: The Kitty Genovese Case*.

It's over and after a horrid down-
pour of mute screams, not even
a hiss or whisper from Kitty G

These are the paper mayors
swelling with the ignorance
of arrogance while grief and
tears get cremated in gray
mornings soaked with rain

As morticians work o-v-e-r-
t-i-m-e to bury another day

And all this happens as feet-
after-feet-after-feet stroll
and rush soundly through
wasted lives - days when

During dinner, Fun City
eats murky conversations

And as the rest cruise in
the Circle Line, hundreds
get murdered in blind streets
and deaf nights full of

D-i-s-t-a-n-t E Y E S

Enraged Rage

NIGHT
Act One

It's dark in your mind
eyes begin to tremble,
lips tighten, waking up
screaming, swallowing

THE PAST
Act Two

His filth attacked your
childhood notions while
thunder cracked the air
exploding in the distance

Beclouded you screamed
but he muted your voice and
laughed fanatically as you
saw mice turning into rats

AND NOW
The Finale

After living in his five fingers
you drink more wine and
hang your feet in midair
while acting on half-a-face

Listening to music stuck to
the walls like monotones
on a shoestring cursing
this razzmatazz

But with the snap of an eye
you dialed for a Ph.D. known
to repair people who had
forgotten how to pronounce

    Beautiful sentences

Love Insurance

How can you ever thank
a best man who slept
with your spouse

    Before he climbed up
    and put himself on
    your cross to forgive

        You for your blindness

How can you ever thank
a woman who bedded
down your brother

    Before she gave
    far more to both
    than to herself

    When the two
    could not even
    espouse to one

        How? You thank them
        with a murdered kiss!

Dark Hooded Phantom

I know you know. You know I know
my mutant face with toxic eyes
is not who you once called Me

I was a peace-loving romantic
before misfortune ripped
apart my wings

My psyche was stuffed in a
laundry bin of hysteria in the
barracks of Nowhere, USA

Where war was a moral poison
profiting from the dead
in the name of globalization

I cut my heart out for America
and returned home to a planet
where technology learned to weep

I sang the PTSD blues
while bombs were still
laughing in my thoughts

I heard my muted comrades
whisper bipolar jokes about
ghost dogs waking up the dead

Before the maggots devoured
the collateral damages. Now all
I want is to cry like a poet

And die like a great actor
under the floodlights of the
World Trade Center Memorial

"Love Always, Minnie"
Prelude to a Déjà vu

I could not imagine finding myself floating in someone else's dream. I was dating my long-time love, recalling how we never ceased to communicate from day one. She had more breaking news than I did. We engaged in family secrets and delicious talk recycled in a million ways—the latest war abroad, health foods, the politics of survival, institutionalized racism and sexism, and fighting for social justice.

We were apart but inseparable. The moment I left her apartment I bumped into things that were not there. No one could take the grin off my face. I got lost but eventually got home when she called. She seemed exhilarated and a bit incredulous, which confused me. She did not succumb to fear unless it meant swimming in rough waters or watching me dash across the street but rarely when the light was green. Her solution: stand still on the corner. Being a Sagittarian speed-walker, this was difficult.

"You won't believe what I found!" she yelled.

"What?" I wondered why she was so animated.

"I found a photo of my sister Minerva aboard a yacht during a vacation in Puerto Rico. She was sitting next to a man with a beautiful suntan. You won't believe who it was!

"Who?" I asked.

"It was YOU!" she shouted.

"Me? But I never met your sister." I responded.

"Come over now and see for yourself!" she said.

I rushed back to her place considering I didn't recall having met Minerva.

Somehow, my *compañera* heard my footsteps and opened the door before I rang the bell. I received a hit-and-run kiss as she rushed to get the photograph while I parked my shoes.

"Look!" she exclaimed. My eyes sank into the stained and faded photo.

"Wow, this is surreal." I replied. There I was—the man with a beautiful suntan.

"Do you remember now?" she implored. Lost for words, I hid in my silence.

"I must have lost my memory in the Bermuda Triangle."

We both laughed, knowing this was my way of abusing bad humor.

"I invited Minerva to accompany me to Puerto Rico the summer after she was hospitalized for depression. I took that picture twelve years ago!" she said.

In the photo, Minerva and I sat near each other but lived worlds apart. The swelling of the aqua green waves danced with our reflections. She turned her back on the sunlight, her soul elsewhere. I was loose and mellow, feeling just as poetic. We were adrift in a Caribbean yacht but in different planets. *And where does the moon go when it's depressed?* I wondered. It all came back to me like pieces of dreams wrapped in cellophane. I felt like a salamander, desperately swimming and flying upstream not certain if a voracious bear waited patiently to devour me.

I snapped out of the nightmare when I heard my *compañera's* voice. "Minnie was a Buddhist who loved psychology, art, and literature," she said.

My eyes were glued to the snapshot, and I recalled we were on Captain One-Eyed Jack's yacht in Puerto Rico. I tried scuba diving and almost got zapped by a school of jellyfish. Luckily, the Captain jumped in and saved me. The sangria he gave me calmed my nerves.

"Look what I also found," my *compañera* exclaimed. "Minerva wrote about critical events that happened in her life after that summer. It's a story of her ordeal and transformation." She opened and read the first page aloud in a soft voice-over:

> For my three beautiful sisters: May each day be filled with the love and sharing described in these pages for as long as we may live. Merry Christmas and Happy New Year! Love Always. Minnie

It was too painful for her to continue.

I asked if I could borrow the brief memoir to write a story-within-a story.

"How are you going to do that?" she asked.

"By reading between the lines," I replied. "Minnie's account reflects a difficult journey of a modern woman in search of her mortality. The unsaid is another story between the lines."

I saw Minerva like a mermaid anchored to my imagination. The sea came to life. She was no longer a mystery to me. I wanted to escape in her words and turn time backwards until Minnie returned home to our seashores. I returned the photo to its place on the refrigerator door. I read and reread Minnie's story. I describe her odyssey as she experienced it. This is her story in my words.

CHAPTER ONE
Reminiscence

I don't know if I was born to be a storyteller who could write about the two cradles of life. I learned that we are all born for a unique purpose. My sisters were highly intelligent and daring. They taught me almost everything about the madness of love. But you can't love all family members or friends in the same ways.

In my case, *Mamí* almost died during my birth. I was her youngest. I had so much to live for, though I was not truly appreciated by my father. I was his last hope of having a son. I was a blessing, a curse, and an outcast from the beginning.

Meanwhile, *Mamí* lived a life worth a great novella. Her parents died when she was eight years old, and she was passed on like leftovers to struggling older relatives who needed a housemaid more than another mouth to feed. *Mamí* survived love and cruelty at the same time. One day as she walked arm-in-arm with her older sister, a man who was obsessed with her, shot her because she did not return his affection. He immediately escaped on horseback and then killed himself. Poetic justice, I guess.

Mamí moved to the Big Apple in 1946 when she was 22 years old. This asphalt jungle was a strange world where people moved as if they had three legs; it was not like in Puerto Rico where even turtles paused to appreciate a kiss from the wind. But she loved the city that never slept.

Four months later, fate stepped in. This was the moment *Papí* froze his eyes on *Mamí,* and he went through several chaperones and maneuvers to get near her. Soon after *Mamí's* aunt and uncle married her off like some trophy brass ring you pluck off a carousel in Coney Island.

After marriage, *Papí* didn't appreciate her; he didn't know how to show love.

My sisters told me whenever *Mamí* heard the loud honking of cars in the street signaling the marriage of a new couple, she would look out the window, and command us to see this spectacle, fiercely declaring, "*Otra que se jodio!*" There goes another woman screwed! I learned bad marriages put women in cages. I was taught never to let a man get comfortable disrespecting you.

I was discovering my own crisis. It was November 11, 1988. I was twenty-five years old. This was the beginning of the end. It was a bitter cold day when I asked, "Leukemia: Who Me?" There were no more guarantees for Happy Birthday! Merry Christmas! And Happy New Year! I felt lost in a beehive of ants and insects dancing with the cosmos. We take for granted that tomorrow is uncertain. For me, it was an illusion of false promises.

For two months or so, I had felt amiss. There was something alien inside me, playing the wrong musical chord. I was slowly crashing into psychosomatic symptoms combined with an infection of relentless pain. My mind lost track of my body.

During this chaos, I was super stressed due to an emotional meltdown. My cousin was dying of AIDS. He was treated like some freak. There was nothing that would be done for him.

In the meantime, I grew fatigued, feverish, swollen with anxiety, aching like a bleeding rock that wanted to cry but too stubborn to admit my fear was painful. The doctors called it a mild infection or anemia. But to me, I felt as if I was preparing for "Death's Audition." And, I was not ready for my close-up!

My Buddhist faith prevented me from falling into a deep hole. My blood test classified me as anemic. My white blood cell count was high. I had to balance work with dieting, health seminars, aerobics, and pushing myself while ignoring what my body was advertising: Take care of your affairs!

I had to take time off from my high-paced job as a pediatric social worker in a neighborhood clinic. I felt guilty abandoning misbegotten young souls who were often treated like the eyesores of society. All I needed, I thought, was one week of rest.

I ignored fear, but it was breathing hard over my ears. I could no longer avoid the possibility that Death was on standby and ready to serve. I felt it in my bones. My Buddhist chants helped me bypass these pins and needles. I visualized and surfed in peaceful thinking. I continued to push myself pretending my body was up to the task. Family and friends arrived with unsolicited, optimistic prayers.

If God were a reasonably priced doctor, I would have hired Him. I had to find someone who could cure me without murdering my finances. I was happy to arrive at Doctor M's office. After completing countless insurance forms that lacked an ounce of empathy, I grew anxious. It took an eternity to fill out these excruciating medical forms. Afterwards, I was directed into a badly decorated office with awful paintings that were boring and heartless. These artworks were guaranteed to kill art critics.

I had a million questions to ask Dr. M when he arrived. He was balding and wore nerdy glasses. Here was God's messenger sitting on a leather swivel chair appearing rather unassuming behind this glorious mahogany desk, while I sweated bullets.

"So, what brings you here today?" Dr. M inquired with a sense of dry humor.

"I need to know what is truly wrong with me," I responded. "Because I've been sick for several months. No one has been able to figure out why."

"Start from the beginning then," Dr. M commanded.

I quickly unfolded a piece of paper with my visits to previous doctors, symptoms, and diagnosis derived. He was attentive to every detail and a good scribbler. I was then escorted into an examining room, handed a one-size-fits-all gown, and instructed to peel off my clothes. I paced awkwardly like a nervous lobster before it was boiled red to perfection. I calmed down when the nurse arrived, but she too wanted to draw blood.

After I was told to get dressed and wait in the reception area.

A while later, Dr. M completed a full exam and shared his outcome: There was the possibility I was suffering from mononucleosis or Lyme disease or it could be something else. "We'll see," he said. "We have to get the blood test results."

Dr. M waved for me to go. He dug deep in his pocket for money and gave it to the record room attendant, instructing him to escort me, and put me in a cab. I was also wondering how I was going to ever pay for this unexpected medical nightmare. *Just hope that Death was not a licensed cabbie!* The tears mixed with humor tasted extra salty. But I was not going straight home. The attendant first took me to the emergency room and my blood slides to the lab.

I was hungry knowing *Mami* was waiting with a homemade meal. She hated bad news. My future was uncertain, and I feared the answers.

I knew something was wrong when Dr. M. called back to see me. My thoughts ricocheted in a pinball machine. I froze in shock denial. Nothing felt coherent. The hunger flew out of my stomach. *Why, me?* I thought. *I'm too young!*

"You need to be hospitalized immediately! You may have leukemia or lymphoma," Dr. M. said.

"Cancer?" I asked while in a complete daze. Dr. M tried to calm down my fears.

"No. It's not the same as cancer," he replied. "But your life span will be reduced if not treated."

To confirm his suspicions, he needed to perform a bone marrow. Everything was moving much too fast. Time pushed against my brain like a shipwreck. I was absorbed with living in a world without me. I was spinning in spiritual confusion. I was shuffled like a deck of cards into an examining room and peeled like a tangerine.

Dr. M asked a nurse to hold my hands, sensing I was freaking out. My eyes didn't pretend. I was a lousy actress, anyway. I was petrified like a child dumped in a closet full of horrific clowns hissing and laughing at me. I sought reassurance, a security blanket, anything that would erase this pain.

I craved for recreational weed. *What were they going to do, anyway! Lock me in jail? I was dying!* Somehow, Dr. M was able to relax my psychodrama. We bonded like two dolphins trapped in a whirlpool of contradictions.

"Do you know who the biggest coward in this room is?" asked Dr. M.

"Me," I replied without hesitation.

"No," he reacted. "And it's not the nurse either." *Okay, who then? Fear!*

He seemed removed from his priggish ways and treated me like a human being, not an insurance claim. We were partners embarking on a very painful journey. I pleaded with him to get all the data he needed so I would never repeat this agony.

Unfortunately, Dr. M was brutally honest and not licensed to make futuristic predictions. Little did I know that bone marrow exams would become a routine part of my life in the coming years.

Dr. M began by positioning me on my side and poking my hipbone for the best location to insert the needle. He instructed me to freeze as he marked the spot with a pen and injected Novocain to numb the area. He waited a few moments before inserting the biggest needle I'd ever seen. I was a lump on a log. He pushed and twisted the needle until it safely entered my hip. I assure you the biggest coward in the room was ready to confess; it was me!

"Let me know when you feel a pulling sensation," asked Dr. M.

"I'm not sure," I replied, "if my pain is pulling, pushing, or twisting."

The nurse clutched my hand tighter as I grit my teeth. I knew that whatever was taking place was worse than I could imagine. Finally, Dr. M informed me he was finished and instructed me to get dressed. I wobbled off the examining table as if rolling out of a meat grinder. I dressed quietly though my state of mind shook like a baby earthquake in angst that no one could feel but me.

I was whisked off to Admissions where I waited hours for a bed. I called my sisters while the slides of my bone marrow were being prepared. We didn't say much. All I wanted was to return home and hide in the bathroom to smoke a blunt.

I would occasionally sneak out to eat or make phone calls. I knew I should call *Mamí. I just didn't have the heart to do it.* I called my older sister and asked her to deliver the news. She didn't want to, but reluctantly agreed. Shortly after, all my sisters and my mother arrived just as I was getting a bed assigned.

Dr. M soon followed.

"We have a lot of talking to do," he declared. I knew then, it was bad news. My sisters, *Mamí*, and I all sat in his office listening to him tell us that I was seriously ill. He would have more answers after the lab tests he said.

I was sent to a room occupied with three elderly women and felt I had been cast in the *Golden Girls* sitcom. I was given a gown, but I refused to wear it. I could not acknowledge I was in the hospital to stay. My fierce sister stood with me. *Mamí* waited in the reception area with my youngest nephew.

My nurse-friend dropped by to say hello. It was she who had recommended Dr. M to me.

"I assure you that you're in the best possible care," she said. "Not only is Dr. M an internist, he's a hematologist who specializes in treating blood disorders."

Without any prior inkling about the nature of my condition, I had definitely ended up in the right place at precisely the right time.

When Dr. M arrived, he closed the curtain and sat on the edge of my bed.

"I have good news and bad news," he said. "It is leukemia, but it's the easiest type to treat and where the most progress has been made."

Dr. M explained that I had the acute lymphoblastic kind that is the most prevalent among children. He proceeded to outline the course of treatment, which included chemotherapy, radiation, spinal taps, blood transfusions, and losing all of my hair. I would be in the hospital four to six weeks.

I was taken aback as I watched a tear trickle down my sister's cheek. She looked away to prevent me from breaking down.

"What if I refuse these treatments?" I asked naively. He looked troubled.

"You would have less than a year to live," Dr. M replied.

I felt like I was slapped across the face without any mercy. *What choices did I really have?* My life turned upside down within a few hours.

"What irony!" I said to my sister. "Me! Who had tried to end my life, would now be fighting for it!"

"You are young. Your life is ahead of you waiting to be lived to its fullest," replied the first-born.

I was still waiting for the good news. Dr. M encouraged me to accept the treatments, which could greatly extend my life. The good news was an offer of hope. He reassured me that I would be able to live a normal life. *Normal?* It was hard to believe.

Still, I didn't cry. No, not until I had to face *Mamí* and confirm what my sister had told her, what the doctor had said that her youngest daughter had leukemia. She didn't understand, but sensed it was serious. When I explained it was a form of cancer, she flew into a rage, insisting that it couldn't be true. It hurt me to see her suffer. That night I hardly slept and cried a storm of aching sobs that I muffled with the pillow, not to awaken my roommates, the *Golden Girls*.

CHAPTER TWO
Hospital Life

The next two weeks were torture. My condition would get worse before it got better. Hospital life required some adapting to. You learned fast there were rules, ethics, and codes of behavior to follow. You are dependent on others to do everything for you. You are frequently treated like a child who should be seen but rarely heard. Doctors would speak about you within earshot as if you were unable to comprehend what they were saying. Many doctors are threatened by your questions of their recommendations; others feel that you're not entitled to a full explanation. You quickly regress to a childlike state of mind.

I had a team of specialists involved in my case, including Dr. M, an intern, a resident, an Oncology nurse, a nutritionist, an infectious disease specialist, and other pros responsible for my chemotherapy protocol. I quickly came to know each one. I had the Hickman catheter inserted into my vein. It was a minor surgical procedure yet frightening for someone who had never been in a hospital. Blood was drawn, and chemotherapy treatments were administered. Since my white blood cells would drop dramatically, leaving me susceptible to every type of infection, I was transferred to a double room.

As an additional precaution, I was confined to my room for a month. Visitors had to scrub their hands, wear facemasks, and sanitized gowns and booties to enter my room. I was forced to take sponge baths over the sink since there was no shower in the bathroom. Hell was loitering in the hallways.

My family came to visit on Thanksgiving Day, bringing an entire feast. I didn't feel I had a great deal to be thankful for. My room was quickly decorated with cards, balloons, artificial flowers, and photographs of all my family members. Friends and relatives poured in daily, bringing books, more food, and good comfort.

"If I had to get leukemia," I said sarcastically, "I was grateful it was at least the best kind." Everyone ignored my blue optimism.

Dr. M entered and informed us that we needed people to donate blood. Recruiting eligible donors became a major project for my family. To my surprise, many people volunteered. The support I received was indispensable. It was at this time I first realized just how much I was loved and who my true friends were.

My Buddhist comrades came to visit often and offered prayers for me when I was too ill to participate. My faith quickly became the single most important factor in my recovery. A modest altar was prepared in the corner of my room where I was able to conduct daily worship. I would awaken early every day to do chanting. I was determined to be out of the hospital by December 24 and circled this day on my calendar. One day, shortly after visiting hours ended, I noticed an unusual amount of activity in my roommate's side of the room.

"What's happening?" I asked a nurse. She directed my question to someone else. I was informed that my roommate had just died of leukemia. I knew she was quite sick, but the possibility she would die so quickly had not crossed my mind. I listened to whispers behind the curtain and saw rolls of bandages and gauze carted into our room.

I lay there, aware there was a corpse lying beside me. I felt fear lingering in the air. An hour later, my roommate's body was removed. I could not fathom how it was possible that just a short while, there was a life in that bed, and now there was none. *Was my fate, moving there?* I spent the next hour frozen in bed and couldn't sleep that night.

Everyone tried to console me by explaining my roommate was much older, and her type of leukemia was not the same as mine. Still, no one could rob me of the awareness that I too was mortal and would die someday, maybe soon. That's not exactly something you think a great deal about when you're twenty-five. I became obsessed with thoughts of death.

My physical condition was deteriorating rapidly. My sense of taste was completely altered, and my appetite was poor. The effects of chemotherapy were beginning to take toll, and I was nauseated every day. I barely had energy to get out of bed some days, though I still prayed. I always made an effort to dress on my own.

On December 1, 1988, I awoke in the morning to discover my pillow was covered with my hair. Although I had been warned about this, I somehow felt I would be the exception to the rule. My dark curly hair had always been one of my outstanding features. Now I was losing my most prized possession. My face was crumbling. I sat in a daze the entire morning until my oldest sister came to see me.

I had asked her to come to cut my hair. As she entered the room, I quickly showed her the pillow, and I burst into tears. She put her arms around me. Tears were rolling down her face as she cut my hair. I'd never seen my oldest sister cry. Nor had there ever been such an open display of affection between us. That moment will forever be engraved in my memory; it completely changed our relationship. We spend the afternoon talking, eating, and playing games to pass the time.

My blood counts were very low that day. I was experiencing nose bleeds. I merely accepted all of these discomforts were side effects of the chemotherapy.

"I'll send a specialist to come see you today," Dr. M said.

Dr. B arrived with one of the friendliest bedside manners I had ever encountered. He proceeded to examine my nostril.

"If you have a certain type of infection, it will need to be treated surgically."

"When?" I asked, knowing I had very little choice in this matter.

I grew accustomed to the torment. He diligently removed some tissue from inside my nose with tweezers and placed it in a solution before he disappeared. When he returned, I heard a great deal of activity outside my room. Dr. M and Dr. B came in. They glanced at my food tray. From the looks on their faces I knew it wasn't good.

"You have a fungal infection called aspergillum," Dr. M informed me.

"It needs to be surgically removed," Dr. B added.

"Why don't you get it over with tonight?" Dr. M continued.

My face told them this news did not sit well with me. Dr. B pulled out a bunch of anatomical charts and began explaining the problem. Before I knew it, I was signing consent forms and receiving a blood transfusion of platelets since I might lose too much blood during the surgery. I was informed that I could not receive general anesthesia because I had eaten throughout the day. I would be awake during the entire procedure.

"The outer part of your nose would not be affected," Dr. B reassured me. "No one will be able to tell you had surgery."

I was placed on a stretcher and wheeled to the operating room. I began to mumble my Buddhist chants under my breath. It seemed the only way to alleviate some of the fear.

Fortunately, Dr. B was sensitive enough to perceive my anxiety. He reassured me by explaining everything he was doing during the process and placed cotton gauze with an anesthetic inside my nostril. My nose grew numb. He asked me to inhale and swallow a solution he said was cocaine.

"You're joking?" I asked Dr. B in disbelief. "I prefer laughing gas!"

He later confirmed that cocaine was actually a commonly used anesthetic for nose operations. I was completely surprised. Then he requested a needle, my biggest childhood fear. I squeezed my eyes shut and chanted silently. I barely felt the needle prick but engraved this in my memory as a living nightmare. The worse part was the sound effects. I heard bones crunching, tissues tearing, and blood spurting.

"How are you doing," Dr. B asked repeatedly.

"Great!" I responded mindlessly.

I was too afraid to stop chanting. When he completed the surgery, he proceeded to pack my nostril with cotton gauze, which made it difficult to breathe. I was wheeled into the recovery room where I was given an oxygen mask. As I lay there, I suddenly felt a surge of joy. I realized if I could get through this, I could survive anything. Perhaps it was the effects of the drugs, but at this moment I experienced an inner peace never felt before.

Dr. B dropped by to see me.

"You did very well," he lauded. I glanced at him drowsily.

"Are you happy?" I replied, with the deepest concern.

"I'm quite happy!" beamed Dr. B.

I realized that the biggest coward in the room was the fear itself. I lost track of time but knew it must be quite late. I begged one of the nurses to call, and let my sister come to see me. By this time, I had a severe rash all over my face; it was an allergic reaction to the platelets. The day had been so long and traumatic for both of us. Fevers and chills bordering on epileptic fits became part of the routine as well.

I sent my sister home, sympathetically. She left, also trying to hide her fear and tears.

Soon afterwards, Dr. B came often to clean my nose, a procedure I dreaded.

"Don't pick or blow your nose," he instructed. "Or sneeze with your mouth open."

The possibility of a recurrence of the fungus was an ever-present concern, which loomed over me. I hated to see Dr. B. His presence would trigger my deepest fears. I would immediately regress to the most infantile state imaginable filled with pleas and tears. "Please find another way to kill the fungus," I begged. He was losing his patience with me, although he did his best to conceal it.

If my white blood count returned to normal, the hope was my body would be better equipped to fight off the infection without the need for further surgery. My face swelled up like a blimp. And my body became the worst place to live—Naraka (Hell) or purgatory.

CHAPTER THREE

Death was my Roommate

For several weeks after the death of my roommate, I had the good fortune of having the room to myself. My eldest sister phoned Dr. M and quickly created a schedule that insured I always had company. Many people came to pray with me for long hours.

My father also came when he learned of my illness. No one would have ever guessed it was the first time we had seen each other in ten years. Miraculously, we quickly connected. He came regularly, always brought food, the newspaper, and was good company. We were getting to know each other for the first time in my life. The rest of my family was equally supportive. They kept close. *I felt home.*

Before long, I had another roommate, also a patient of Dr. M's who suffered from leukemia. Perhaps he hoped this elderly woman and I would inspirit each other, especially since she was just beginning the treatments, and I was near completing the first phase of mine. She immediately objected to my Buddhist practice and visitors who came to chant with me and complained to Dr. M. I was angry with her interference in the one thing that gave me strength and courage.

I was determined to show her what Buddhism was about through my actions. I was even more compassionate towards her. I awoke extra early while she was still asleep and prayed quietly until Dr. M arrived. When she was awake, I would hide in the bathroom and chat for as long as I needed. I offered prayers for her well-being. I was regaining some strength but was not allowed outside my room since my white blood cells were going up.

Meanwhile, my roommate began her treatments. I observed that her experience was similar to what I had been through. I did everything I could to make her feel more comfortable as she struggled with nausea, drowsiness, blood transfusions, and everything else that came with leukemia. I would help her dress, fetch her water, tidy up her night table, and answer phone calls. Never did I begrudge her when she interfered with my religious practice.

We spoke often about our experiences and discovered we lived within blocks of one another! Her son had recently died of AIDS. I told her that my cousin was sick with AIDS, and we encouraged each other. When you find yourself alone, the world is without you. No book, pet, or houseplant can ever replace the emphatic listener. I shared the gifts I was born with and helped her to let go of the skeptic.

On December 15, 1988, Dr. M performed the fifth, and the most crucial bone marrow exam to determine if I was in remission or not. I requested some form of sedation to subdue the fear of the uncertain. I waited for Dr. M to return with the results. He arrived with a smile that said it all.

"You're in remission," he said proudly. "There are no longer any detectable leukemia cells."

We enthusiastically slapped hands like two kids in grade school. Yet the uncertain was not over. He told me I needed to continue aggressive treatments and regular bone marrow exams for at least two years.

"To insure you remained in remission," Dr. M emphasized.

I knew it would be a long haul, not a long shot. But at that moment, I could only bask in the joy of knowing that I had survived the first major hurdle. I would be home soon. It was the best Christmas present I had ever received.

But I also began to panic about going home. I realized just how co-dependent I had become on my doctors. I wondered how I would manage without the daily monitoring at the hospital. I worried my body would secretly begin to produce leukemia cells again, and if I would be able to manage the care of my Hickman catheter on my own. Dr. M used his light sense of humor to constantly reassure me.

I began to prepare myself for going home and planned what I would wear since the winter was upon us. I used my remaining time at the hospital to make hand-made holiday cards to give to all who helped me through this crisis. I gave some to nurses, aides, and doctors who were supportive during my stay. I never thought I would be so glum leaving the hospital and saying goodbye to so many people. *Yet, this was exactly how I felt.*

On December 24, 1988, six weeks after being admitted, I felt badly that I would be home celebrating the holidays with my family while my roommate would spent Christmas alone in the hospital. I gave her a card and a small gift that morning. She thanked me and said she would open the gift on Christmas Day. Her radio had not been working and, knowing how much she loved classical music, I fixed it and replaced the batteries from my own radio.

She thanked me warmly, "You have given me the best present." We said farewell, and I rushed to meet my sister who was in the corridor waiting to take me to my family.

We arrived at my older sister's apartment, and I slowly entered the living room. All the guests were already there—my mother, sisters, niece, nephews, and a few friends. I saw a huge sign on the wall, "Welcome Home, Minnie. We Love You." I was moved by this open display of affection. The festivities began with a hearty meal, music, picture taking, and sharing of gifts. My father came to this gathering.

It was the first time in so many years that the entire family was celebrating Christmas together. In some awkward way, I felt there was some purpose to my horrible illness, if this was what it took to see my family united. I experienced this holiday season in a completely new light. I was appreciative of the small things I once took for granted. I was aware for the first time just how important I was to every member of my family. The guests began to trickle out into the dark, winter night carrying bags of gifts and many heartwarming memories.

I went to stay at *Mami*'s house. She and I lived in the same building, so it was easy for me to have access to my apartment when I needed. Everything seemed different—everything even simple things like waking up, taking a shower, brewing tea, grabbing things, walking through the streets and feeling the cold, shopping or just tagging along with a list of things to do; all felt like extraordinarily new experiences.

I realized what being confined to a hospital for a long period of time could do to you. You lose a little of who you were, before and after, when you return home.

CHAPTER FOUR

An Elusive Promise

There were no more ordinary days in my life. I had to reinvent myself. I slept with a nightlight and stared at the ceiling for hours. At times I got lost in my thoughts. *I desperately told my mind to stop telling me what I was thinking!* It was getting me into troubled waters without any bridges to cross. When I finally fell asleep, I dreamt I was a little girl in an orphanage for leukemia. I awoke with a jolt and bathed in sweat. I had many dreams like this almost as if I were having nightmares in a sealed coffin. I began to chant with my eyes closed and listened to the echoes of tranquility to overshadow my despair.

When I didn't have an appointment, I spent my time at my mother's place, watching "I Love Lucy" reruns and game shows. *Anything to calm my mind.* The idea of being alone for a moment was too frightening. I sought refuge in the security of my mother's home. I depended on her cooking, doing my laundry, bathing me, and taking me to appointments. I felt like a reborn child. It took quite some time before I could manage these tasks on my own.

Still, living with my mother made it impossible not to get stuck in the past. She learned to smile much more, and it peeled off the pain from my face. We ceased to be perfect strangers. *Mamí* gave us the heart to work smart, depend on no one, and crave for everything. My outlook about *"No Place like Home"* was never the same.

I spent weeks racing back and forth to the hospital. I stayed three full days getting my amphotericin and chemotherapy. Dr. M spoke to me about a bone marrow transplant as the next step in my treatment. It's a relatively new procedure involving transfusion of healthy bone marrow from a compatible donor. Although success rates were high, the procedure was not free of considerable hardships and risks.

My sisters were tested for compatibility, and two qualified. I was fortunate since many people in desperate need of transplants were unable to find a suitable donor.

The transplant entailed being confined to an isolation unit for months without any natural defense system to help combat infections. I was overwhelmed by this decision. Worse, there was still no guarantee. I may have a relapse in the future. It was difficult to accept the idea of subjecting one of my sisters to repeated bone marrow exams while I was under general anesthesia. This was the method used to gather sufficient marrow for my transplant. I needed more time to make a decision that I could live with. Time was not waiting for me, anyway.

On January 8, 1989, two weeks after my discharge, I began having high fevers. My blood count had been low for several days. I was immediately readmitted to the hospital. It was a shattering disappointment. I hoped my return home would mark the beginning of a recovery. Instead, I awoke to find myself right back where I started.

I began to think about my former roommate. C.M. was her name; she came to mind.

"How is C.M. doing these days?" I asked Dr. M.

"Not good," he replied, somewhat annoyed I had inquired.

"I was thinking of calling her," I responded.

"Don't!" he said abruptly.

I didn't press the issue but wondered what was happening. I later learned that my roommate had died shortly after I was discharged. I was heartbroken. I remembered the intimate weeks we spent together and was grateful we bonded during her last days. I wondered if that nonchalant attitude I misunderstood for confidence wasn't just a quiet resignation to her fate. Was spending the holidays in the hospital more than she could bear? Or, was it her son's death that left her feeling living was not worth the fight? I strongly believed that desire to live plays a major role in one's recovery.

I now understood Dr. M's discomfort. Rather than be angered, I was filled with affection for him. Health professionals vow to preserve life. They struggle with time, life, and death. I never brought up the subject of my roommate again. I realized Dr. M's intention was to spare me further pain. It also magnified my preoccupation with my own destiny. Would I follow the same footsteps as my previous roommates? *Was I to be Strike Three?*

On January 16, 1989, I celebrated my twenty-sixth birthday. A chocolate cake with candy was delivered from the hospital cafeteria. I opened presents and indulged in ice cream before slipping into a delirium of raging fevers and uncontrollable chills. I desperately tried to maintain a positive frame of mind but grew increasingly depressed as the day wore on.

My sisters visited that evening and did their best to cheer me with more presents and jokes. My sullen face didn't know how to let the sun in. I cried as I held my sister's hand. Everyone shed tears. Frustration stuck in our hearts.

"I feel like I'm running a marathon race," I confessed. I'm past the first few miles and already slowing down. I'm tired and don't know if I could get to the finish line."

I huddled and hid under the covers.

"Please, don't give up!" My oldest sister pleaded, squeezing my hand tighter.

I was torn between my desire to give up and not wanting to cause my family suffering. After a painful silence, they left quietly. I drifted into sleep while singing under my breath, "Happy Birthday" to me.

The next day, *Mamí* came with a strained look with which I was only too familiar. She broke down and told me that my cousin had died of AIDS. I heard that everyone turned their backs on him, fearing exposure to this horrific disease. They called AIDS — "God's Curse."

I remembered when he visited me at the hospital, and how he cried, confiding he might not last until Christmas and worried about his mother who stood by him when others wouldn't. The news of his death was more than I could stand. I caved in and cried long and hard. My thoughts were getting me into trouble again. It had been after this final encounter with my cousin that I began to get ill. Some people close to me whispered that perhaps I had contracted something from him. We were excommunicated like lepers. I felt a sense of camaraderie with him. I hated the damaging gossip behind closed doors.

I spent the next several days, questioning everyone about the details of his funeral. His greatest desire was for Judy Garland's "Somewhere Over the Rainbow" to be played at his funeral. I had fulfilled his final wish and spent the next several weeks, listening to this song ad nauseum:

> Someday, I'll wish upon a star and wake up where the clouds are far behind me. Where troubles melt like lemon drops. Oh, way above the chimney tops, that's where you'll find me…"

I found some solace in these words and felt my cousin spoke directly to me through the lyrics. Still, the news of his death combined with the reality of my own illness, contributed to my declining morale and increasing depression. I succumbed to having higher fevers without detectable causes. The most renowned medical specialists were baffled by my case. I seriously began to question whether I truly wanted to continue waging this battle. Was it worth it? I completely lost my will to live, stopped chanting, and felt life slowly slipping from me.

I confided in Dr. M about these feelings. Instead of receiving expected sympathy, I was met with some brutally honest words: "You know what I think," said Dr. M. "That you're being selfish. You have a family that loves you, and who is supportive and worried about you. How would they feel if you gave up? You'll still young and have a lot you can do in life. Stop feeling sorry for yourself!" He admonished me severely, quite callous in his candor. I felt angry and misunderstood. Perhaps underneath it all, he really didn't respect me. I cursed him as he left the room and continued to do so in my sleep. I felt so alone. I had not felt this type of loneliness in a long time.

I later came to appreciate Dr. M's honesty. It became my greatest incentive to recover from this illness. Dr. M played his cards right and pushed the punk in me, straight out of the room. That evening I received my Buddhist friends, and we chanted together endlessly while I broke into a sweat, which lasted for many hours. I was inspirited for the first time in weeks and that night, my fever broke.

On January 28, 1989, I was discharged from the hospital. I prayed it was the last time. I was relieved to exit from this environment. I quickly realized, however, that this battle was just beginning. The immediate crisis might be over, but I still had two years of treatments ahead and a whole new life to reconstruct. I had no idea where to begin.

Perhaps the future was an elusive promise. Sigmund Freud once said:

> Follow your dreams! You only get one life and make sure it's the best damn life you can make it.

Somehow, my oldest sister sensed I needed time away from this ordeal. She invited me to join her for a Caribbean vacation in Puerto Rico.

"I'll think about it."

"*Mamí* loved *La Isla del Encanto*. It is where the moon goes to, when it is blue."

AND FIRE

The Blood of the Poet

It was 1952 when we escaped an island
    Invaded with bombings, mass hysteria
And bloody massacres and came to an
    Inner city that Mama called *Noo Jork*.

When we reached the baggage terminal,
    Mama saw our luggage sprawled over
The cold floor. It was the first time I'd seen
    A proud, passionate rose sighing
While melting inside snow.

It was a time of great prosperity yet fear
    For newcomers daring to hope that
America embraced you as part of its
    Own national soul, not as migratory
Sponges and domesticated pets.

We were treated like flying cockroaches
    Or atomic bed bugs who spoke poor
Puerto Rican English with a Bronx accent.

To think American, Mama reasoned, we
    Ate peanut butter and jelly sandwiches
While dressing less tropical to blend in
    With the typical-lite Dick & Jane.

"Your first In-glish lesson," she warned,
      "Forget about yellow rice with pigeon
Peas and avocados. Say: *Hamburger with*
      French fries and ketchup, Pliz!"

My siblings and I learned English by
      Reading the eyes of strangers to see
If the classmates were friendly or cold-
      Blooded assassins whose smirk was
A daily public execution with loathing.

If you spoke Spanish, you were dead meat,
      Left stranded in the corner of the world
With a dunce cap on my head and I went
      Home with a bilingual headache.

Perhaps if my cinnamon face was shown
      In Norman Rockwell's paintings of
Americana, I may not have been treated
      Like some nonentity called me *Other*.

I came to school to stretch my mind, not to
      Face a firing squad of stuffed shirts and
Baby gum racists whose mucus membrane
      Missed the evolution highway. It was a
Blatant conspiracy to color me invisible.

With patience and humility, Mama once
      Believed, true faith was at its best in
The dark. Her mantra was an eye-opener
      To this ten-year-old with pensive eyes.

It freed the fearful soul, converting a cold
      Chill into sweet molasses. And the left-
Handed rebel poet with tenacity was born.

I wrote about why silence came from stones
     And turned darkness into light. My pride
Was intolerable when I made my pencil talk.

I was a poet without a country when I was
      Stamped culturally deprived and hood-
Winked into comatose and moronic classes
      Where learning was a dead-end dream.

If you were magnificent at mumbling,
      Sleeping on your desk or looking out
The window for the inner grasp of outer
      Space while scratching your cupcakes,
You were the class genius or top clown.
      No rock deserved this miseducation.

I went from ghetto kid — who read comics
      And the dictionary like Bible study, got
Hip with street smarts and mixed martial
      Arts to avoid being a warlord for young
Savages with a switchblade temper — to
      Swank intellect who knew a poem went
Deeper than a bullet with your name on it.

It was 1965. These were the years when
      Death came at an early age and youth
Went to prison and sadly mistaken it for
      A motel. I was in my twenties and just

As clueless about the ways of lovers with
    Roving eyes whose foxy hearts played
The game face more savagely than I did.

I made a vow after witnessing so many
    Shotgun weddings to zip it before a
Captivating muse convinced Mama that
    She was the last virgin in high school
With this murderous confession.

It was painful to see the children left in
    The cold when the sperm-donors left
The keys dangling on the door before
    The coffee grew bitter; they were out
And gone way before nightfall.

My other choices were a one-way trip to
    The Vietnam War with a *Return To
Sender* dog tag in my lead coffin stuffed
    With a duffle bag of weed; or escape to
NYU, where I was first called "Brother."

These were the definitive times of dogma
    And rigidity turned into dissent when
Free love and peace were a plus, and not
    A cockfight for John Wayne's America.

We struggled with the burden of so many
    Memories that became protest songs of
Overcoming a world of laughing bombs
    Gone mad - while the brave and noble
Were liquidated when they were moved

By conviction and acted with resolve:
The quest for perfection is social justice.

My age of discovery was the *Birth of the*
    Cool when jazz went vogue in America,
Knowing every rhythm had its dark side,
    Where only the self exists when *Blues*
People play with Black fire to change the
    Expectations of the world.

When I heard Miles, I saw this matador
    With a horn and a bloody rose in his
Mouth, serenading a sullen bull; while
    Coltrane was the spirit-seeker whose
Solace was in the sounds of emotions to
    Dismantle any notion of conformity.

I searched for my roots while hanging
    Loose with Blake, Lorca, Willie Shake,
Amiri Baraka, Neruda or Langston Hughes,
    Dancing mambos with metaphors
While Puertoricanizing America.

When I graduated with my intellectual
    NYU pajamas in Madison Square
Garden, Mama asked me to return to
    The Bronx when it was still burning.
When I knocked on the door, she didn't
    Know if I was Jesus or Che Guevara.

The Immigrant's Tale

I am a descendant of the Mother of
Exiles: An immigrant of weavers
Whose roots from the Old Heartland
Saw the world as a loom and used
The imagination to be one's destiny.

Most seafaring dreamers were purged
By vicious monarchs who treated us
Like slaves, putrid cheese or thieves.
We were born in painful debt and
Wealth was an alluring mistress.

We were carried by an enormous
Wind of adventure, grit and risks,
And we clung to hope to survive
The storms of humble beginnings.

We were the mules or wetbacks
Chained to the cruel machines
That catered to an abyss of
The ultra-rich and vile!

I am that hungry refugee walking
Among the shadows - that street
Vendor with a load of humor
And irony bearing witness to the
Moronic hatred and privilege
Fears of the unknown.

We are still a labor of love
In progress.

The Undesirables & Unstoppable

I
On the Other Side of the Border Wall
"The Migrant Curse"

On the other side where time flows
Back home in slow motion between
Raging mystic rivers, checkpoints,
Misty mountains and border walls

Nature is an equalizer and
The Indigenous spirit of the
Wretched poor can't silence

The brutal storms of grinding
Poverty or sexual violence as
Taxation and escape the dirty
Little wars, the extrajudicial
Executions and death screams

Of maddening hunger stuck in
The ribs of Newborns crushed
Like recycled beer cans for
The lowest at the totem pole

While the seasons of neglect and
Alchemy of human grief continues
Caravans of immigrants who ride
An iron horse called *The Beast*

They always have a story to tell
Cause every mile is different
And these migrants are the
Kissing cousins of the universe

II
Once Inside / Still Outside
"Backpacks for Sale!"

These are the new pioneering
Foreigners in No Man's Land
Who are maligned and vilified
As demented and deprived in

The flagship propaganda
Of Trumpmania, USA:
The Forbidden Nation

They seek a paradise of great
Expectations with ludicrous
Ideas and momentous dreams
Of one made from many who

Left behind abandoned families
And starving communities
Where the hardships lack
The seeds of radical hope

And roads of forgotten
History repeats itself

Until they're ready to embark
On a near-death experience as
Refugees and asylum seekers
Left waiting in concentration
Camps to dehydrate in hell

And cut off from the world

Only those who took the wrong
Road at the worse time knew a
God's prayer was the last meal
Before the vultures waited
To eat their imagination

Oh, the juggernaut of it all
And tyranny of inhumanity!

III
"Giants Throwing Stones
& Tear Gas at Ghosts"

Who suffers and struggles more:
Those who cross the border or
Those who stayed behind

It is a sickness in the head not
To provide for your own
While harvesting false hope
Like a poisoned crop
Of rotten memories

Once caught you are dog food for
The political pimps and savage
Capitalists who grudgingly give
Canned spray cheese and
Frozen scorn sandwiches
With gratuitous contempt

After all, who needs soap,
A bird bath and a toothbrush
After surviving a scalding desert

When you could depend on the
Wrath of the global power elite
And its sidekick Fascist goons
To persecute you wholesale
With born-chilling anxiety

Why do many risk everything
And nothing to be stigmatized
And purged as racialized scabs
With such pristine impunity

There are no spared words for the
Medicated hatred spewed upon
Those who break through or fly
Over steel walls to desperately seek
Work, freedom, peace of mind

And bear their own
Children of glory

Cool Chameleon

I was born with a face only
A lineup of unusual suspects
Could ever recognize.

To those with small eyes
I'm an Outsider
Anchored in America.

Every birth is a migrant:
I am not violating the
U.S. Constitution.

I have the right not to be
Profiled or detained like
Some felon *Made-in-Prison*.

I am not a Stop sign—
I was born free at first
And not at last!

I have the right to be silent
When you expect me to guess
The whereabouts of your mind.

Which is why I shift gears
Knowing my face is still
Behind your self-denial.

JULIA de JULIA

It has to be from here,
right this instance,
my cry into the world.
"Farewell in Welfare Island"

You were born ahead of the times
at the brisk of dawn and died
anonymously shortly after
midnight in a full-time jungle
where loneliness stood naked
in broad daylight.

You were found unconscious
like some discarded torn
handbag without a name on
a cold-blooded pavement
in Spanish Harlem.

No one filed a missing
person's report. No one
came to the morgue.

You were buried in Potter's Field
like a decayed bronze flower
who arose from the bitter
dust of a tormented moon
drunk with tears to bless

The insatiable soul of the
poet with a kiss of water.

A month later, you were
exhumed and repatriated,
returned to a hero's
welcome in a stolen
homeland you had
fought to free.

Your dreams-in-water said it all:
you slept in the rhythms of the
clouds whose mysteries cried
on your breast and lay to rest
wild passions knowing a
lover's deceptive kiss is
a woman's Achilles' heel.

You were not born to fit
the mold of a mistress who
became a disposable muse
that was tamed and bridled
like some tortured soul
dancing with humiliation.

You knew Death was an
unfaithful lover who tried
to ravage your gifts with
a bouquet of illusions.

Yet you refused to be a
treasured starfish! A violin
of anorexic despair!

You were born restless in
the brisk of dawn, defiant
and just as rebellious as a
revolutionary with justice
as your code of honor.

Only the Poet could restore
one's soul by giving Death
a complete refund.

Welcome to life,
Julia de Burgos!

Aphrodite's Wisdom

I was a goddess the moment
I broke the chains of patriarchy
when absorbed by how others
were attracted to me.

I grew tired of uncaring lovers
who promised the world or
how to lasso the moon but
couldn't even tie their shoes.

Worse were those who roared
like ferocious lions in the streets
with more thorns than roses.

I was that rebel whose mind
ran much too fast to stand still
frontal and dead center
like a warped Picasso.

I refused to be the predator's
trophy in a catwalk jungle of
scandalous snakes in Hollywood.

Truth to power: These serial rapists
will no longer get away with murder!

Person #000

Are you not tired of returning
To the shadows of guilt—
That silence killing you
Like some wild pet
Kept in a zoo?

Was your residing in prison
Where death is a layaway plan
With no legal holidays in hell
An addiction to living stupid.

What crossroads led you
In the wrong direction
When you ran backwards
To kiss the future.

Was it falling blindly in love
With enablers who laughed
As you partied ad nauseam
And blacked out in despair.

Who abandoned whom!

Was your childhood thrown
Out with the garbage like
A crazed Marvel toy
Desperate to be a man!

When will you cease to pour
A thousand apologies in a
Barrel of cheap beer and
Cry like a human again.

Was it when the children
Learned to pray for you
In the dark and whisper
Your name in absentia?

The laws of self-sabotage
-Reap what you sow-
A one-way ticket behind
Prison bars with deep rage.

Do not expect to heal while
Sitting on both hands if you
Left your emotional pain
In a safe deposit box.

Instead, create a flag of
Peace from those who
Love you most and return
Home under liberated skies.

Mad Dog Blues

Dizzy came from the old school
Of mad dogs returning home
From a war killing anything
And everything that moved

This soldier promised himself
If he survived this madness
He would return to Harlem
Where deep-fried souls
Crossed the streets with
Steel hearts singing gospel
And surrendered to the blues

Like born-anew virgins

You can't kill relentless faith
Born from the spirituals of
Stardust and many rivers

And turn our prayers into
Invisibles shadows under
A demonic moon

Bessie, Ethel & Billie were hip
To those Jim Crow years when
The hypocrisy of whiteness
Was a motherless child

You improvised and survived
Between love and fear
Or sang and played it
Between hope and despair

Like never heard before

The Anonymous Thinker

The moment Omar entered an
American university like
A mystical UFO in black

He had to hide his thoughts
To free himself from this
Tyranny of arrogance

Omar was to walk unseen
Among those who played
Blind with his wholeness

He was that odd one in
The mix who kept alive
How xenophobia had

Imprisoned free will

Omar earned his post-doctorate
In racial integrity and
World peace with

A sense of wonder

Anatomy of Hatred

The imperial wizard drove
My shrink to tears last night.

He probed into Duke's devil
-May-care of others' misfortune for
Having forfeited their lives in
The pursuit of freedom.

Duke was wired for Jim Crow in
The Deep South when priests
Used the pulpit to provoke
The hatred of blackness.

His savage mind was
Painted pure white taking
Great pleasure stepping
Over the voiceless
And the damned.

Duke's intolerance was
Homemade hatred.

The shrink asked,
"How do you sleep
At night?"

The swastikas in his eyes
Told the shrink the hater
Would have hated more
In his sleep and brag about it
Without any remorse
Or fake apology.

There were no tears or
Love lost between them.

Only disbelief.

I am Erica Garner!

I am a woman of many lives
and a great-grand-daughter
of those conceived by rape

Born on a cotton plantation
and forced to resist the
trauma of oppression.

I am the strong backbone
of Sojourner Truth and
wings of Harriet Tubman.

We lost those lynched and
hung from poplar trees
and bodies left burnt crisp
in shallow graves.

Many protests and battles
still pour from the scorn and
brutalization of generations.

I am the arch and bond of
these immortal tears who
survived turbulent times.

I am before and beyond
the chokehold cries of
Black Lives Matter.

I am pure vintage blackness
with an unapologetic will to
overcome the relentless pain
of chronic fatigue syndrome.

I left this world how I lived it:
screaming from the top of
my lungs for social justice!

Oscar is Everywhere but Home

The memory of our pain
deserves to be appreciated,
remembered, and never denied.
— Oscar López Rivera

Oscar is everywhere but home.

I saw a cardboard of him
Standing on a terrace in
Old San Juan, wearing a faded
Beige sweatshirt, khaki pants
And pain-free sneakers.

An awarded Bronze Star Vietnam
Vet and anti-colonial combatant
This patriot was ambushed in an
American court full of rightwing
Zika mosquitos and viciously
Sentenced for seditious conspiracy.

Oscar was put in several U.S. gulags
Where robotic guards thrived on
Cooked up ways to drive this
Dissident insane or kill himself.

They tried everything in the book of
Absolute torture, bitter isolation,
Catcalls and sensory deprivation

To destroy this freedom fighter
With radioactive hope.

Oscar called this severe mental
And physical agony *spiritcide*.[1]

Why was this "Mandela of the
Americas" so dangerous to
The U.S. penal wastelands
And its toxic existence?

Because Oscar refused
to be on his knees
*¡Cuando los cogió
con la mano en la masa!*

Gringolandia was caught
Red-handed in the act
Of colonial oppression!

A bona fide revolutionary
Can't be neutralized or
Rehabilitated, America!

Even death stood aside and
Closed its eyes when Oscar
Dared to think out of the box

---

1. Oscar López Rivera, *The Torture of Imprisonment*. (PM Press, 2013).

And get a Caribbean whiff
Of the aqua green sea and
Kiss the blue sky of his
Beloved homeland.

Mind you, we still protest
And march until Oscar
Eventually returns home.[2]

---

2. Since Oscar López Rivera's incarceration in 1981, activists and supporters have organized to obtain his release. The "Free Oscar" campaigns achieved victory on January 17, 2017 when President Barack Obama commuted the 55-year sentence. Oscar returned to Puerto Rico on May 12, 2017 to a jubilant national celebration. He remains active in struggles for the decolonization of his homeland.

The Storm, the Hurricane and the Rebellion

"Don't you realize that the Sea is the home of water?"
– Zora Neale Hurston

Hurricane María sprung
from a breezy wave in
Africa and it grew as
a tropical storm until
her explosive intensity
ravaged Puerto Rico.

The seashores were
homeless and sudden
death was hidden over
widespread nightmares
of sadness and shock.

After the hurricane there
were no maps on hand.
No celestial spheres. No
greenery in the mountains.
No vegetation in the fields.
No rainbow or blue horizon.

Everyone was cast away
like a shipwreck of fear
drowning in darkness.

You wake up to see what
is there but not there.

María transformed an enchanting isle,
shaping it like an industrial omelet
of unforgivable rainfall, mudslides,
toxic water and twisted roads.

Our landscapes were ripped in
disbelief and scattered prayers.
We didn't have a moment of
silence for silence to have
a moment of its own.

We belonged to the wilderness
of water and barren trees and
slept under a murderous sky
in baby-blue tarp seashells
once called home.

The sea inside us was an insecure
heart trading winds between hope
and despair while our dreams
drifted behind clouds of lost
memories where time once
fell asleep in peace.

The devastation was unimaginable.
Nearly five thousand were no
longer the salt of the earth while
the aging, bedridden and dying
held on to dear life.

María was apolitical and didn't
know that La Fortaleza was
the playground of parasites
and U.S. colonial puppets.

Bloodsuckers shed no tears for
the dead, only malicious intent.

A hurricane doesn't know if
poverty and world hunger
is a humanitarian crisis or
a political problem.

María wouldn't know if a bird
held in captivity could fly in
the wild and create a song of
freedom with its own wings.

A natural disaster wouldn't know
if the tears of the skies could be
wiped by flying paper towels.

María had no idea the global power
elite built wars in your backyard;
or the Jones Act made Puerto Rico
an American cash cow.

What POTUS called a great rescue
mission, we call a flea market of
bonds reduced to junk status for
U.S. millionaires licensed to kill
the poor to privatize our future.

María revealed the immoral cruelty
of those who failed to plan and
who were much too slow
and who never cared.

Those who survived had each other's
back with the passion of rebuilding.
Many organized brigades of communal
relief without any need for permission.

They were the holy water of patriotic
dissent who gave every pueblo its
magic to dance with hurricanes
and sing in rejuvenated spirit.

The Puerto Rican diaspora
responded with resourceful
hearts and the loving
was just as abundant.

It didn't matter if you were a
real American with benefits or
famously Puerto Rican with
a decolonized mentality.

María forced us to listen and
use our collective voices to do
what others never could.

An artist painted the Puerto Rican
flag in open plazas and shattered
walls to bring light, recyclable
faith and life back home.

He sketched the veins of resilience
and invited the people to color
the sky with a liberated mind.

Maria prepared the people for the
July rebellion when half a million
protesters took to the streets.

The governor's unforgivable
chat exposed his misogyny,
homophobia, and disdain
for the people.

He proposed feeding his cows
with the refrigerated cadavers
waiting for a proper burial.

People gathered, grew stronger
and were no longer afraid of
holding destiny in their hands.

The mass pride of unity was forged
in radical change and struggle
against imperial oppression.

They came to protest on horseback,
motorcycles and in kayaks to
reclaim their country while
toppling those who had
fallen out of favor.

The governor was forced to resign!

People united in a revolutionary
awakening so that our voices
would no longer be silenced
or pushed into exile.

La Patria rose and it refused
to be Puertoricanless!

"Somos más y no tenemos miedo."

¡Que viva Puerto Rico libre!

La Tormenta, el Huracán y la Rebelión

*"No te das cuenta que el
¿Mar es el hogar del agua?"*
-Zora Neale Hurston

Todos somos como el mar:
salimos a una jornada
a volver a nosotros mismos.

El huracán María surgió
de una ola brisosa en África
y creció como una tormenta
tropical hasta que su intensidad
explosiva destruyó a Puerto Rico.

Las costas quedaron sin hogar
y muerte súbita escondida
por amplias pesadillas
de pena y espanto.

Luego del huracán no
hubo mapas a la mano.
Ninguna esfera celestial.
Ningún verdor en las montañas.
Ninguna vegetación en los campos.
Ningún arco iris u horizontes azules.

Todos fueron lanzados afuera
como en un naufragio de miedo
ahogándose en la oscuridad.

Despiertas a ver lo que
está ahí pero no está ahí.

María transformó una encantadora isla
dándole forma de tortilla industrial
de imperdonable lluvia, alud de lodos,
agua tóxica y carreteras torcidas.

Nuestros paisajes fueron rasgados
en incredulidad y rezos al viento.
No tuvimos un momento de
silencio para que el silencio
tuviera un momento suyo.

Pertenecimos a la salvajada
del agua y árboles pelados
y dormíamos bajo un cielo
feroz en toldos azules como
a manera de conchas marinas
una vez nuestro hogar.

El mar dentro de nosotros era un
corazón inseguro con vientos alisios
entre esperanza y desesperación
mientras nuestros sueños detrás de
nubes de memorias perdidas donde
el tiempo cayó dormido en paz.

La devastación fue inimaginable.

Casi cinco mil ya no eran
la sal de la tierra mientras
los envejecientes, encamados
y moribundos se agarraban
a la querida vida.

María era apolítica y no sabía
que La Fortaleza era un patio de
juegos de parásitos y marionetas
coloniales de Estados Unidos.

Los chupasangres no lloraban
por los muertos, solamente
tienen maliciosa intención.

Un huracán no sabe si la pobreza
y la hambruna mundial
es una crisis humanitaria
o un problema político.

María no sabría si un pájaro
en cautividad podría volar libre
y crear una canción de libertad
batiendo sus alas.

Un desastre natural no sabría
si las lágrimas de los cielos
se podrían secar con rollos de
papel toalla tirados al aire.

María no tenía idea de que
la poderosa elite global
construyó guerras en tu patio,
o que el Jones Act hizo a
Puerto Rico en una
mina de oro americana.

Los que POTUS llamó una gran
misión de rescate, nosotros llamamos
una pulguera de bonos chatarra para
los millonarios de Estados Unidos
con licencia para matar a los pobres
y privatizar nuestro futuro.

María reveló la inmoral crueldad
de los que fallaron planear
y que fueron muy lentos
y nunca se preocuparon.

Los que sobrevivieron se cuidaban
las espaldas con la pasión de reconstruir.
Muchos organizaron brigadas de apoyo
mutuo sin necesidad de permisos.

Ellos eran el agua bendita de los patriotas
disidentes que dieron a cada pueblo
la magia de bailar con huracanes
y cantar con el espíritu rejuvenecido.

La diáspora puertorriqueña respondió
con recursos del corazón y la
a morosidad así de abundante.

No importaba si eras un americano
de verdad con beneficios
o famoso puertorriqueño con
una mentalidad descolonizada.

María nos obligó a oír y usar
nuestras voces colectivas para
hacer lo que el gobierno
nunca podría.

Un artista pintó la bandera
puertorriqueña en plazas públicas
y derrumbó paredes para traer luz,
fe reciclable y vida de vuelta a casa.

Dibujó las venas de resistencia
e invitó al pueblo a colorear el
cielo con una mente liberada.

María preparó a la gente para
la rebelión de julio cuando más
de mitad de un millón de
protestadores tomó las calles.

El imperdonable chat del gobernador
descubrió su misoginia, homofobia
y desdén por el pueblo.

El propuso alimentar sus vacas
con los cadáveres congelados
esperando decente sepultura.

El pueblo se arremolinó y se
crecieron fuertes y no tuvieron
temor detener el destino
en sus manos.

El orgullo de unidad masa se forjó
en un cambio radical y luchar
contra la opresión imperial.

Vinieron a protestar a caballo,
motocicletas y en kayaks para
reclamar su país a la vez echar
abajo a los caídos en desgracia.

¡El gobernador fue obligado a renunciar!

La gente unida en un despertar
revolucionario para que nuestras
voces no fueran más silenciadas
o empujadas al exilio.

¡La Patria se levantó y rehusó
estar sin puertorriqueñidad!

"Somos más y no tenemos miedo."

¡Que viva Puerto Rico libre!

Acknowledgements

Poetry has many little lives before emerging as an assortment of spontaneous whispers, "callings", and visualizations in a book. I am inspired by beautiful minds whose literary and visual gifts as cultural workers serve to uplift universal souls.

My heartfelt thanks to artist Rudy Gutierrez for the brilliant book cover and interior art in *Heartbeats, Rhythms, And Fire*. His vibrant images combine the elements of a cosmic mythological surfer who paints in whirling strokes with six hands to embrace the labyrinth in the blood of the poet. This Boricua renaissance artist has a kaleidoscopic view that translates poetry into storytelling and magic realism. It has been a great honor and privilege to jam with this humble sage and visual poet. I am grateful for his friendship, love, genius, and collaborative spirit.

I am also blessed with the love, encouragement, patience, and guidance of Iris Morales, publisher and editor of Red Sugarcane Press. Her steadfast vision and editorial gifts challenged me to break new ground and seek new directions. I appreciate her honesty, artistic integrity, and constructive feedback. Iris' creative and practical suggestions gave *Heartbeats, Rhythms, And Fire* its design, poetry selections, and literary enrichment. This book is as much her vision and dreamscape as it is mine.

I am indebted to poet and Africana Studies Fulbright Scholar Melba Joyce Boyd for writing the Foreword: *Identities, Nations, and Literary Movements*. I am especially thankful that Melba enthusiastically committed to reading my manuscript and adding her poetic wisdom. Thank you, Sista' Melba, for your support in giving my poetics its raw wings. Your literary analysis made this book more transformative.

I want to express my gratitude to poet, professor, and editor Alberto Martínez-Márquez for his insightful *Reflections of a Scholar*. I am thankful for his support in Puerto Rico where he continues to provide a literary consortium, voice and a stage for writers. *Mil Gracias, Poeta!*

I want to thank the following poets and visual artists for their support, insights, and comments — Peggy Robles-Alvarado: a feminist muse, educator and activist; Magdalena Gómez: a playwright and the poet laureate of Springfield, Massachusetts who is truly indomitable; Amina Baraka: poet, activist and blues singer extraordinaire; George Malave, a master visual artist who prefers talking to invisible people; Pedro López Adorno: scholar, editor and a poet who knows the rhythms of water reflect the natural history of the senses; and artist and scholar Juan Sánchez, whose multi-media art has paved the way for his disciples to embrace their cultural roots as a means to build community. I am deeply grateful to José Olmo Olmo for his Spanish to English translations of *Reflections of a Scholar* and *The Storm, the Hurricane, and the Rebellion*; and to my dear friend Gilda Rivera-Pantojas for her valuable feedback.

I thank Dr. Victor G. Alicea, President of Boricua College, and my esteemed colleagues who encouraged and supported me throughout the writing of this book.

About the Author

José Angel Figueroa was born in Mayaguez, Puerto Rico but grew up in the Southeast Bronx, New York. He is a poet, playwright, actor, editor, and professor. A master of poetic storytelling, visual imagery, and metaphor, Figueroa is best known for powerful social commentary related to the Latinx experience, the colonial oppression of Puerto Rico, and the exploitation of people of color in the United States. Among his books are: *The Invisibles* (coauthor George Malave), *A Mirror In My Own Backstage, Un Espejo En Mi Propio Bastidor, Hypocrisy Held Hostage, Noo Jork*, and *East 110th Street*.

An early writer of the Puerto Rican experience in New York, Figueroa was a major contributor to the Neorican literary movement and the original Nuyorican Poets Café, and is credited in *The Norton Anthology of Latino Literature, Harvest of Empire: A History of Latinos in America, The Hispanic Condition: Reflections on Culture & Identity in America*, and *The Nuyorican Experience*. His writings have been internationally translated, published, and widely anthologized in *Aloud: Voices from the Nuyorican Poets Café, Bum Rush the Page: A Def Poetry Jam, Papiros De Babel: Antologia de la poesía puertorriqueña en Nueva York, Red, White, and Blues: Poets on the Promise of America*, and *Puerto Rican Writers at Home in the USA*, among others.

Figueroa was awarded the prestigious *Premio Educación, Poeta* from the Instituto de Puerto Rico in New York in 2014 and the *Por la Literatura y la Paz con Justicia Social* by La Unión Hispanomundial de Escritores in Puerto Rico in 2015.

Also known for his work in the theater, Figueroa wrote, coproduced, and directed *A Tribute to the Life and Times and Work of Piri Thomas,* a multi-arts presentation at Hostos Community College in New York. His play *Transnightification* was directed by his mentor Raul Julia at the Joseph Papp's Public Theater; and his jazz opera *King of the Crabs* was performed at Intar Hispanic American Theater. He also produced and directed the critically acclaimed *The Grassroots Poets Series* at Miriam Colon's Puerto Rican Traveling Theater.

Figueroa has worked with students and adults in public schools, colleges and universities, community venues, and prisons. He has taught poetics, drama, creative writing, English, African American literature and teacher education curricula at several U.S. universities. His work as a children's literature specialist, language arts consultant, and poet/artist-in-residence with New York State Poets in the Schools, Teachers & Writers Collaborative, and Poets & Writers Inc. resulted in the design, editing and publishing of numerous anthologies of original children's poetry and youth writings in statewide public schools.

Presently, Figueroa is a professor of Puerto Rican, Latin American and Caribbean literature at Boricua College in the Bronx.

About the Artist

Rudy Gutierrez is an award-winning artist and illustrator. Gutierrez's work has been described as "Wall Medicine," ancient yet contemporary, urban in a sense, and musical in feel. He is known for creating images that combine elements of indigenous art with those of urban culture. His artwork for periodicals, books, magazines, records, CDs, films, and paintings have been exhibited and distributed worldwide.

Gutierrez feels that an artist's highest honor and fulfillment is to inspire and uplift. To this end, he has offered his work for numerous causes and continues to do so. He has performed as a guest artist doing live painting, backdrops, stage props, workshops, and benefit concerts for organizations working with youth and bringing artistic opportunities to them. Gutierrez contributed art to the First Annual Anti-Apartheid show at the United Nations, participated in a touring show in Germany exploring social issues, and donated art to the International Cultures Foundation.

Many of Gutierrez's works illustrate musical themes such as the cover artwork for Carlos Santana's musical recording, "Shaman," which was also used as a set design at the 2002 Super Bowl half-time show and on various promotions to fight AIDS in South Africa. He also created the U.S. Postal Service Forever Stamp for the Musical Icon Series of Jimi Hendrix. Gutierrez's paintings of John Coltrane, originally used for the book *Spirit Seeker-John Coltrane's Musical Journey*, were commissioned for the film, *Chasing Trane: The John Coltrane Documentary*. His work was featured as the curatorial spotlight for the "Jazz it Up" exhibition at the Mesa Contemporary Arts Museum in Arizona in 2019.

As part of the "Proyecto Raices," Gutierrez created art to be reproduced as murals in cities across the United States that were presented and seen in Miami, Dallas, and Los Angeles. His anti-domestic violence painting "Shelter" was viewed in the film, "The Task." Gutierrez exhibited at the World Conference Against Racism in Durban, South Africa. He also contributed and co-curated "The Prevailing Human Spirit" exhibition at the Society of Illustrators in New York in a benefit for the victims of 9/11.

Among his many publications, Gutierrez is a contributor to *The Education of an Illustrator and Teaching Illustration*. His art is featured in *Art Revolution: Alternative Approaches for Fine Artists and Illustrators* and in *Star Wars Visions*, showcasing several artists selected by George Lucas.

Gutierrez has been widely recognized for his impressive art and talent. His numerous awards include the Dean Cornwell Recognition Hall of Fame, Distinguished Educator in the Arts, and a Gold Medal from the New York Society of Illustrators. His children's books have garnered him a Pura Belpré Honor, Américas Book Award, Children's Africana Book Awards-Africa Access Award, and a New York Book Award, among others.

Gutierrez has lectured and conducted workshops nationally and abroad and is a tenured professor at Pratt Institute where he has taught since 1990. He was born in the Bronx, New York to Puerto Rican parents and raised in New Jersey.

About the Editor

Iris Morales is a lifelong activist for social justice, racial and gender equality, and the decolonization of Puerto Rico. Her love of community, history, and storytelling has led her to wide-ranging collaborations on these issues with activists, writers, and artists, and to the founding of Red Sugarcane Press.

Morales has compiled, edited, and published several important anthologies including *Voices from Puerto Rico: Post-Hurricane Maria* about the impact and intersection of climate disaster and colonialism, and *Latinas: Struggles & Protests in 21st Century USA*, a collection of contemporary Latina writers and feminist perspectives.

Morales is the author of *Through the Eyes of Rebel Women, The Young Lords: 1969 to 1976*, the first account of women members; she was a leading member for five years. Her essays and articles have been published widely in anthologies, journals, and online magazines. Morales is also the producer, writer, and codirector of the award-winning documentary, *¡Palante, Siempre Palante! The Young Lords*, initially broadcast on national public television in 1996, which continues to be screened in classrooms and community venues across the United States and the Caribbean.

Morales is an attorney, a graduate of New York University School of Law, and holds an MFA in Integrated Media Arts from Hunter College.

For more information www.irismoralesnycwordpress.com

About Red Sugarcane Press

Founded in 2012, Red Sugarcane Press is dedicated to presenting and documenting the rich history and culture of the Puerto Rican and Latinx Diasporas in the Americas. It publishes authors whose diverse writings and voices break new ground, inspire, deepen our knowledge about history, promote dialogue about contemporary affairs, and entertain.

Red Sugarcane Press publications include poetry and prose collections, narratives and stories that reflect the passions and convictions of working people's lives, especially untold or forgotten stories from the journeys of indigenous and African peoples in the Americas who from enslavement to the present have triumphed through the courage and tenacity of many generations.

www.redsugarcanepress.com
www.facebook.com/RedSugarcanePress

www.ingramcontent.com/pod-product-compliance
Lightning Source LLC
Chambersburg PA
CBHW052210090526
44584CB00016BA/2043